Victor Hugo's
LES
MISÉRABLES

Lawrence Klibbe
Professor of Romance Languages
New York University

1998 Barnes & Noble Books

MACMILLAN is a registered trademark of Macmillan, Inc.
Monarch and colophons are trademarks of Simon & Schuster, Inc.,
registered in the U.S. Patent and Trademark Office.

Macmillan Publishing USA
A division of Simon & Schuster, Inc.
1633 Broadway
New York, NY 10019

ISBN 0-7607-1096-1

Text design by Tony Meisel

Printed and bound in the United States of America

98 99 00 01 02 03 M 9 8 7 6 5 4 3 2 1

RRDC

CONTENTS

INTRODUCTION TO VICTOR HUGO

Victor Hugo was born in Besancon, France, on February 26, 1802, and died in Paris on May 22, 1885. His lifetime thus spans the nineteenth century, a period that has been called "The Century of Victor Hugo." The varied and controversial literary and political movements of the age are reflected in his works, and he forcefully represents the prevailing beliefs in science, democracy, and liberty. Hugo overshadows his contemporaries by his vast output of his pen; the authoritative edition of his writings comprises forty-five volumes.

YOUTH

Victor Hugo's early years coincided with the "Age of Napoleon." The future writer's father was an officer and later a general in the French Army, and Hugo's early childhood was spent in Paris and abroad, as he traveled with his father to such places as Corsica (1803), Naples (1808), and Spain (1811). His formal education, however, took place in the French capital, and he attended excellent schools, such as the famous lycée Louis-le-Grand (1816–1818), which is an approximate equivalent of an American high school and junior college. In 1817 he won an "Honorable Mention" award for poetry from the French Academy, and this surprising literary triumph for a boy of fifteen determined him on a writing career. In his notebook, he wrote: "I will be Chateaubriand or nothing." Chateaubriand was the leading French writer during the early nineteenth century.

EARLY SUCCESS

By 1819, Hugo had won prizes from the Academy of Toulouse and from the French Academy; and he founded, with his two brothers, a magazine called *Le Conservateur littéraire* (1819–1821). But the death of his mother in 1821 and his father's the unsympathetic reaction to his requests for money to support a writing career brought about the end of the magazine. Nevertheless, in 1822 Hugo published *Odes,* and the poems were widely acclaimed in government and literary circles. Chateaubriand praised the young man who aspired to his laurels, and King Louis XVIII granted him an income. That same year, he married his childhood sweetheart, Adele Foucher, and began earning his affectionate title, "Papa Hugo," with the birth of four children in 1824, 1826, 1828, and 1830, respectively.

LEADERSHIP OF THE ROMANTIC SCHOOL

At this time, Europe was caught in the onrushing tides of Romanticism, that literary and political reaction against Classicism, which urged freedom and liberty as the principles of art and life. In 1823, Hugo wrote a "Gothic" novel, *Han d'Islande*, which emphasized the grotesque and frightful as a reaction to the well-ordered world of the Classicists. In this work, Hans, the horrible monster, slays his enemies with a stone ax and drinks the blood from a human skull.

Hugo also composed poetry with more tranquil themes of the Romantic Movement. His poetry achieved increasing popularity with the public and with the young Romantics. Books such as *Nouvelles Odes* (1824), *Odes et Ballades* (1826), and *Les Orientales* (1829) secured his leadership among the struggling poets of Romanticism. As a critic, he won fame with another magazine, *Muse francaise,* which lasted only about one year (1823-1824), but gathered about Hugo many able young writers. By 1827, Hugo was considered the chief of the embattled Romantics through two efforts: the formation of the *Romantic Cénacle* (literary circle) at Hugo's home, and the publication of the *Préface de Cromwell*.

The *Cénacle* brought Hugo into contact with Sainte-Beuve, perhaps the most formidable literary critic of nineteenth century France, and with all the ideas and exponents of Romantic doctrine. The preface to the play *Cromwell* is far more important than the drama itself: Hugo urged the Romantics to accept Shakespeare as their model; and he advocated freedom from the three unities of time, place, and action. He also upheld the mingling in the same work of the tragic and the comic, the grotesque and the sublime. The preface resulted in an uproar, and the Romantic battle was joined in the area of the theater.

ROMANTIC TRIUMPH

Hugo now had to defend his theories in practical form: he had to write a play which would follow the rules of the *Préface de Cromwell*. In 1830, the famous "Battle of Hernani" occurred. Hugo wrote this play, *Hernani,* utilizing Spain as the background that fitted the doctrine of the exotic, mysterious, and medieval as proper "Romantic" subjects. *Hernani* violated almost every possible classical rule; for example, Hugo shifted the stress of the lines from the rigid formulae of Corneille and Racine, the seventeenth-century French dramatists, to a variety of emphatic measures. In fact, this last innovation started the "battle" between the two sides. The classicists hooted and howled at the very first line of the play which showed this change. Théophile Gautier, a famous writer and witness of the event, wrote: "Two systems, two parties, two armies, it is not too much to say two civilizations confronted each other, hating each other cordially, as one hates in literary quarrels, and ready to swoop down on each other." The play lasted forty-five performances, a very respectable figure at that time, and the classicists finally yielded, accepting the drama. Hugo was unanimously hailed as the slayer of the classical dragon. Romanticism triumphed now in all genres.

MORE ROMANTIC VICTORIES

Victorious first in the area of Romantic poetry and now in the Romantic theater, Hugo devoted his time to continuing his work in these genres. His poetry added luster to his already well-established name, and he wrote five more Romantic dramas between 1831 and 1835. The height of his victory in the drama came in 1838 with *Ruy Blas,* another play set in Spain. The novel was the only literary form he had not conquered, although he had penned an early effort, *Han d'Islande* in 1823. He now channeled his energies toward this genre, at least partly out of necessity; for one thing, he had signed a contract in 1828 to write a historical novel, and the manuscript was due within five months of the signing. As a result of the editor's howls of complaint, Hugo at last started to write the book in late 1830, and the novel was published as *Notre-Dame de Paris* in 1831. Translated into English as *The Hunchback of Notre-Dame,* this novel won Hugo perhaps even more popularity than his masterwork, *Les Misérables.* The melodramatic story of Quasimodo, the monstrous bellringer of the cathedral, and the picturesque setting of Notre Dame and medieval Paris were instantly captivating to an audience hungry for Romantic tales. Hugo himself defined the work as a "work of imagination, caprice, and fantasy."

Unopposed as leader of the Romantic school, Hugo now stormed the bastions of the French Academy. Repulsed in 1836 twice in his bid for membership, and again during 1839–1840, he finally secured a place in 1841 by the narrow vote of 17 to 15.

POLITICAL COMMITMENT
The ten years from 1841 through 1851 marked the Hugo's political education and commitment. Although Romanticism, by its advocacy of liberty and freedom in literature, was also linked closely to the winning of these ideals in the political arena, Hugo had veered dangerously close to the conservative and monarchical viewpoints during previous years. He had showed himself attracted to the cult of Napoleon Bonaparte around 1831, to liberalism between 1832 and 1835, and to the July Monarchy of Louis-Philippe (1830–1848) which had the support of the *bourgeoisie,* or middle class.

In fact, the Duke of Orléans had supported his bid to the French Academy; and in 1845 Victor Hugo was named a Peer of France. But during the Second Republic (1848–1851), Hugo committed himself completely to the democratic and liberal ideals that he followed the rest of his life. In 1848 he was elected to the National Assembly and at first tried to steer a moderate course between the urgent demands of the suffering proletariat and the bourgeoisie. For this reason, he spoke and wrote for the candidacy of Louis Napoleon Bonaparte, nephew of Napoleon I, as president of the French Republic. His doubts about the former's imperialistic ambitions were subdued by a tendency to compromise until 1851. Then Hugo saw the results of his early folly in following a dictator bent upon total power: Louis Napoleon wanted to destroy the Republic and become the emperor of France as Napoleon III. In the three years of compromise and silence, Hugo saw that France was now willing to follow Louis Napoleon. By the time Hugo was determined to denounce the dictator, all popular support was lacking.

EXILE

Nevertheless, on July 17, 1851, Victor Hugo delivered a bitter attack in the National Assembly against Louis Napoleon. He angrily said that "because we had Napoleon the Great, must we have Napoleon the Little?" This famous phrase, *Napoléon le Petit,* became the rallying cry of Victor Hugo against Napoleon III for nineteen years. Orders for Hugo's arrest were signed on Dec. 3, 1851, after Napoleon III had crushed all resistance to his coming conversion of France into an empire. Hugo fled first to Belgium, where his continuing political activity forced that government to urge his departure. After a few days in London, he settled definitively on the Island of Jersey in the English within sight of the French coast. He composed a book of satirical poetry, *Les Châtiments,* in 1853 against the French Emperor, in which he predicted very accurately that Napoleon III would lead France down the road to defeat. Hugo depicted Napoleon

III as a thief, a tyrant, and a coward. However, the tides of political fortunes were flowing in favor of his enemy: England and France had become allies against Russia in the Crimean War, and Hugo's attacks were embarrassing to the British government. In 1855, he was compelled to move to the island of Guernsey near Jersey where he was likewise ordered to stay out of the foreign affairs of England.

RETURN TO LITERARY ACHIEVEMENTS

While this latest blow stifled his Channel—political activity, at least openly, the years at Guernsey were a period of intense literary achievement. Hugo had observed and learned much about human nature, men in power, and the political struggle of the nineteenth century. By the terms of his new exile on Guernsey, he decided to express in literature the profound truths he had acquired at great cost. The poems in *Les Contemplations* (1856) are completely divorced from politics; the lyrical and philosophical aspects predominate in the themes of nature, love, and death. In *La Légende des siècles* (1859), Hugo endeavors to write a historical and philosophical poem about the progress of mankind through the centuries. By refusing to go along with the dictatorial plans of Napoleon III, Hugo had sacrificed a substantial income of about 60,000 francs a year and had been required to live rather frugally. Thus for Hugo, the reduced income from his writings was a necessary substitute for his political idealism, which had caused him financial losses. He could have returned to France because Napoleon III announced a general amnesty for all his foes in exile, but Hugo stubbornly proclaimed that either Napoleon III or he would have to live in exile—and since the former seemed securely in power in Paris, Hugo would remain abroad. Hugo wrote: "True to the engagement I have made with my own conscience, I shall share to the end the exile of Liberty. When Liberty returns, I shall return."

LES MISÉRABLES

Hugo's courageous stand allowed him time to compose his acknowledged masterpiece, *Les Misérables,* published in 1862. He had been working on the manuscript, *Les Miséres,* prior to 1848 when he actively entered politics. Now, in exile in 1860, he had taken up the project in great earnest. He wrote that "Dante created a hell out of poetry; I have tried to create one out of reality." This book of more than twelve hundred pages was almost immediately recognized as the novel of the nineteenth century; both critical and popular acclaim came to Hugo at the age of sixty when he had seemed to be on the sidelines of the new literary movement of Realism. Perhaps the brief preface to the book is the best initial clue to his aims and beliefs: "So long as there shall exist, by reason of law and custom, a social condemnation, which, in the face of civilization, artificially creates hells on earth, and complicates a destiny that is divine, with human fatality; so long as the three problems of the age— the degradation of man by poverty, the ruin of woman by starvation, and the dwarfing of childhood by physical and spiritual night—are not solved; so long as, in certain regions, social asphyxia shall be possible; in other words, and from a yet more extended point of view, so long as ignorance and misery remain on earth, books like this cannot be useless."

RETURN TO FRANCE

After nineteen years, Hugo's warnings about the disasters that the dictatorship of Napoleon III would bring proved accurate. In 1870, France was quickly and completely defeated in the war with Prussia, and Napoleon III surrendered the cream of the French army at Sédan. It was now the turn of "Napoleon le Petit" to go into exile. Although Hugo returned in triumph to France as the prophet vindicated, he could not enjoy his trip back. He saw the nation in defeat and hastened to Paris where he pleaded uselessly with the Prussians to make peace with the new French Republic since the Second Empire had collapsed. He then exhorted the French to continue the fight, was elected again to the National Assembly, and strove for a just peace between France and Germany. He wrote: "No more frontiers! The Rhine for all! Let us be the same Republic, the United States of Europe. . . . Let there be universal peace! And now let us shake hands, for we have rendered service to each other; you have delivered us from our emperor, and we deliver you from yours."

When Germany demanded acceptance of a harsh peace treaty and France immediately began to plan revenge, Hugo wrote prophetically of the future of Europe: "There will be henceforth in Europe two nations to be feared: one because it will be victorious, the other because it will be vanquished." The increasing bitterness between Frenchmen on the Left and on the Right further disillusioned Hugo, who strove to achieve a stable government. At last, he ironically left France again, this time of his own accord, and went back in 1872 to Guernsey where he had spent so many years gazing at his native land in the distance.

LAST YEAR
In 1873, Hugo came back once more to Paris and was elected to the Senate in 1876. Still the old warhorse of politics, he fought any possible signs of a new dictatorship. For example, he helped to block the growing ambitions for more power of Marshal MacMahon who had been chosen president. After 1878, he continued to publish, but the works had been written at earlier dates. It is of course impossible to list even all the major works of Victor Hugo, but one must bear in mind that he had produced important literary efforts in the midst of intense political action. For example, he wrote two symbolic novels, *Les travailleurs de la mer* (1866) and *L'homme qui rit* (1869) during the years of exile as well as *William Shakespeare* (1864), a critical essay which revealed more of Hugo's thought than that of the English dra-

matist. In 1874, Hugo published a historical novel about the French Revolution, *Quatre-vingt-Treize;* and in 1877 appeared a continuation of *La légende des siècles.*

On the occasion of his eightieth birthday, Hugo was eulogized by his countrymen as a national hero. However, his health was gradually failing, and his role in literary and political activities was clearly at an end. In the summer of 1883, he left the following indications as a form of last testament:

> I give 50,000 francs to the poor. I wish to be carried to the cemetery in their hearse. I refuse the prayers of all churches. I believe in God.

In spite of his wishes for a simple burial, Hugo's death occasioned a period of national mourning, and the funeral ceremonies were marked by unparalleled pomp and circumstance. Maurice Barrès, the French novelist, wrote that: "The scene had to be seen to be believed. . . . A mass of people eddied and flowed from as far away as the Place de la Concorde, pressing forward against the barrier of terrified horses to within two hundred yards of the catafalque. There was, in them, a wild wonder at the knowledge that they had made a god. . . ."

CONTINUING FAME AND CRITICAL REPUTATION

Although critical reaction after his death in 1885 has not always been kind to Victor Hugo, his importance has certainly been recognized by his fellow poets. André Maurois, biographer of Hugo among others, states that "other poets, Baudelaire, Mallarmé, Valéry, have been thought to attain to a greater perfection, and indeed, because of the strict and novel standards which they set themselves, have frequently done so. But without Hugo they would never have existed at all, as they themselves have admitted." One of these poets, Paul Valéry, a major poetic influence in the twentieth

century, confirms this statement: "He was the very embodiment of power. . . . To get a clear view of his stature, one
has to realize what the poets born within the climate of his
influence had to invent in order to be able to compete with
him at all."

On June 10, 1952, the 150th anniversary of his birth was
celebrated in Paris, and France paid devoted tribute to the
memory of Victor Hugo. "Never," writes André Maurois,
"has a nation been so closely knit with one single body of
writing." While Hugo may not be deemed a dominant influence on the writers and in the literature of contemporary
France, he is genuinely regarded with respect as the man
who most nobly represents the French spirit of the nineteenth century. He also epitomizes in *Les Misérables* all the
political, social, and literary problems and ideals of that era.
Foreign impressions of this situation obviously have been
formed by the novel, as can be seen in the many translations
in all countries since 1862.

For American readers, Victor Hugo is probably little known
as a poet and dramatist outside academic circles. As a novelist, he is familiar to American audiences mainly through two
works, *Notre-Dame de Paris* and *Les Misérables*. The first
novel, with its thrilling, melodramatic action and exotic, romantic descriptions, has a basic appeal in plot and setting.
However, there can be little doubt that the second novel is
superior in terms of characters, ideas, and philosophies. *Les
Misérables* still contains valid and useful ideals of goodness
and humanitarianism for the quest of man toward progress
and enlightenment.

BRIEF SUMMARY

Jean Valjean is an ex-convict, sentenced to the galleys for stealing a loaf of bread to feed his widowed sister's family. Imprisonment has made him hard and angry. He steals silver from a good bishop, but the bishop tells the police it was a gift. Through the bishop's redemptive love, he is transformed into a good person who rises to be mayor of his town under the name M. Madeleine. But he is watched by the police inspector, Javert, who remembers him as a convict. Working for Madeleine is a young woman, Fantine has an illigitimate child, Cosette, whom she has placed with a couple. When Fantine becomes ill, Madeleine tries to help her, but she dies.

Madeleine learns that an innocent man is being imprisoned for a petty crime he committed. He turns himself in and goes back to the galleys. But he escapes and once again begins a new life. He finds the badly neglected Cosette and cares for her, while trying to stay one step ahead of the implacable Javert.

Cosette grows into young womanhood and falls in love with Marius. Valjean knows he must give her up, but she has been his whole life. In the uprising of 1832, Marius is badly wounded, and Valjean risks his life to save the young man. He carries Marius to safety through the Paris sewers. But the act is costly for Valjean: he falls into Javert's clutches. Valjean asks to take Marius, who is all but dead, home, and Javert agrees. Valjean's heroism has shaken his belief that criminals are the essence of evil. He lets Valjean go, but unable to live with the decision, commits suicide.

Marius recovers and weds Colette. Valjean confesses that he was once a convict, and Marius repudiates him as a thief

and a murderer. Then Marius learns that he has misjudged
Valjean, and that Valjean saved his life. He and Colette go
to Valjean, who is ill. With his loved ones nearby, he dies
happy.

DETAILED ANALYSIS
PART I: FANTINE

BOOK ONE

In the year 1815, Bishop Myriel has served the diocese of D____ since 1806 and is widely admired by all the people for his exemplary conduct. This man of seventy-five personifies the essence of saintly conduct by his kindness and charity; he lives so modestly that it is difficult to recognize his rank as a bishop. One of the tenets of his life is that prejudice and vice are the real sources of evil and that "the great dangers are within us." In short, he warns that "we should fear ourselves."

COMMENT

Bishop Myriel is one of the outstanding characters of this novel although he only appears in the first two books of this part. This ecclesiastic represents one of the two great themes in the novel: the innate goodness found in mankind. He also expresses several of Hugo's attitudes, such as the need for popular education. However, the portrait of the old bishop was drawn initially from a certain Msgr. de Miollis who befriended a recently released convict seeking shelter when the whole neighborhood refused help. To the outcries of some scandalized readers who resented this adaptation, Hugo exclaimed: "There is in *Les Misérables* a bishop who is good, sincere, humble, paternal, who is intelligent as well as gentle and who mingles all virtues in his benediction. That is why *Les Misérables* is an infamous book." The reader must accustom himself to accept and understand Hugo's realism at the outset of the reading of this very long novel: long and detailed descriptions of the historical background of the youthful period of Bishop Myriel's life; many examples of the man's idealism and noble conduct; and the exact verbal rendition of the physical setting.

BOOK TWO

Jean Valjean, freed after nineteen years as a galley slave for stealing a loaf of bread, enters the town of D—— in October of 1815 and is denied food and shelter by the terrified inhabitants. Now forty-six years old, Jean Valjean is an embittered and desperate man who finally comes to the bishop's house for aid. Bishop Myriel receives him warmly, has dinner served the former convict, and personally shows Jean Valjean a comfortable bedroom. However, Valjean is tempted by the sight of the bishop's silverware and escapes with it during the night. He is swiftly apprehended and brought before the bishop, who states that the silverware was a gift to Valjean and that he should also take the two silver candlesticks. Alone with Jean, Bishop Myriel wants him to use the silver to become an honest man. In a speech which will haunt Jean the rest of his life, the saintly old man explains that: "Jean Valjean, my brother: you belong no longer to evil, but to good. It is your soul that I am buying for you. I withdraw it from dark thoughts and from the spirit of perdition, and I give it to God." Nevertheless, Jean suffers one more relapse into evil: he later encounters a boy with a coin and puts his foot upon the money when it rolls near him. Rejecting the youngster's pleading, Jean keeps the coin. Remorse overcomes him, and he seeks out the child and weeps bitterly that he cannot return the money.

COMMENT

This highly dramatic episode is crucial to the entire novel. Without Bishop Myriel's faith, Jean Valjean would have killed him during the night he stole the silverware. Goodness is not enough in itself because the bishop demands redemption from Jean Valjean. The former convict must become a good man and save other people from evil and suffering. Thus, the bishop's philosophy of humanitarianism is not merely passive but active. If evil can be contagious, so may goodness spread just as readily. The struggle is not decided easily, and Jean's wavering at sight of the sleeping bishop is the first positive victory of charity. The theft of the coin from Petit Gervais is a realistic touch which stresses the enormous mental agony of Jean Valjean. Nevertheless, goodness wins, and Jean's weeping and subsequent kneeling in the street before the bishop's house are the decisive and conclusive steps in his salvation. The whole episode is of course a forceful denunciation of the merciless and unjust penal code of the day. Hugo's stirring narration of Jean Valjean's crime and punishment is a bitter attack upon a society which allowed men to starve and then imprisoned them for stealing some bread. Hugo likewise condemns the smug and uncharitable citizens who failed to help a fellow human being in his plight.

BOOK THREE

The scene is Paris in 1817. Four young men of the middle class meet and start to woo four girls of the working class. They obviously have no intention to wed the young ladies. Fantine falls in love with Tholomyès and is seduced by him. The gay blades return to their families and leave the girls without any remorse. However, Fantine is pregnant.

COMMENT

Hugo describes Paris during the beginning of the Restoration under Louis XVIII. On the surface, society is polished and civilized, but there are the many injustices being done to the poor and to the laboring classes. The four young men represent the power of money and position; they enjoy life without any concern for hurt feelings. The young women, particularly Fantine, are simple, naive country damsels who are overwhelmed by the fine manners and gallant airs of the flirtatious middle-class gentlemen. The contrast between the classes is sharply and ironically depicted.

BOOK FOUR

Fantine, unable to support Cosette, her illegitimate child, leaves the three-year-old child in the care of the Thénardiers at Montfermeil, near Paris. Hugo succinctly describes the Thénardiers thus: "The woman was at heart a brute; the man a blackguard." However, Fantine is unaware of the true character of the guardians of Cosette and pays them well from her meager wages. Cosette is so mistreated that at the end of three years with the Thénardiers, her mother would have had trouble recognizing her.

COMMENT

It is important in the later development of the plot to keep in mind that Thénardier plays constantly on the fact that he was a sergeant at the battle of Waterloo in 1815. Hugo also contrasts the goodness and innocence of Fantine and Cosette with the cruelty and ugliness of the Thénardiers. An appeal is made directly to the emotions of the reader in the miserable treatment accorded to Cosette and the continuing woes of Fantine.

BOOK FIVE

Fantine has been working at a place called M____ sur M____, (Hugo often conceals the exact place names in episodes of the novel). At the end of 1815, a laborer arrived in the town and set up a small factory; the town has enjoyed great prosperity, and the citizens call this stranger Father Madeleine. It is obvious as Hugo reveals the humanitarianism and charity of Father Madeleine that he is really Jean Valjean, putting into practice the lessons he learned from Bishop Myriel. For example, the news of his benefactor's death in 1821 plunges Father Madeleine into great sorrow and arouses the ever-present curiosity of the people. Father Madeleine likewise refuses honors such as the offer of the post of mayor until the position is forced on him.

Only one man resists the magnetic appeal of Madeleine: Javert, the inspector of police. Javert, born in a prison, has become the implacable defender of the law; he has only two goals in life, respect for authority and hatred of rebellion. For one thing, Javert is sure that he has seen Madeleine previously. One day, an old man, Fauchelevent, fell under his cart and before a jack could be brought, he would be crushed. Madeleine had destroyed Fauchelevent's business in the town by his own, more efficient business sense, and Fauchelevent was Madeleine's foe. However, Madeleine uses his back as a lever to lift the cart, and all the bystanders are in awe, except Javert, who states coldly to the mayor that he knows of only one man capable of such strength—a galley slave. Thus, Madeleine has risked his own security and safety to live in the light of kindness and love.

Meanwhile, an old busybody, Madame Victurnien, has discovered about Fantine's child and succeeds in getting the unfortunate mother discharged from her job—in Madeleine's factory. However, the former Jean Valjean is unaware of this situation. Fantine slips into degradation in her efforts to earn money for Cosette's upkeep; at last, she is only a prostitute. For example, she has sold her hair and even her two front teeth for money. When a provincial dandy makes fun of her ugly and pitiful appearance and throws snow down her back, Fantine reacts violently; but in the ensuing struggle, Javert arrests her. She is sentenced to six months in jail, but Madeleine enters the courtroom and commands Javert to "set this woman at liberty." At last, Madeleine confronts Javert: kindness faces authority. Madeleine explains that Fantine was innocent and only defended herself. Javert stresses the defense of the citizen against insult.

Fantine is overwhelmed by the angry scene between the mayor, whom she mistakenly blames for her plight that started when she was fired from his business, and Javert, whom she does not know whether to trust or fear. Finally, Madeleine explains to her that she will work no more and that Cosette will be brought to her.

COMMENT

Although a relatively brief book and lacking in the digressions and explanations which have been observed already in the novel, this fifth book is a crucial element in the entire work. The two great protagonists, Jean Valjean and Javert, meet; and the chase is on. This pursuit-and-flight theme will be found throughout the novel.

It is important to analyze carefully the opposing viewpoints of the two men. These views are more than personal differences; they are the essence of Hugo's criticism of the political and social world of the Restoration and the Industrial Revolution. Javert represents law and order, and the privileges of the bourgeoisie in their quest for money and power. Hugo is attacking the monarchy for fostering such an attitude as part of national policy. Jean Valjean symbolizes the liberal and religious ideals which valued the individual and protested against suffering. For instance, Hugo writes in this fifth book: "What is this history of Fantine? It is society buying a slave. . . . The holy law of Jesus Christ governs our civilization, but it does not yet permeate it."

Consequently, there are the two levels of interpretation to be recalled in the struggle between Jean Valjean and Javert: the personal or psychological, and the philosophical. Hugo also employs the familiar Romantic device of the grotesque versus the beautiful. Fantine, on the surface ugly and reprehensible, is really good and laudatory because of her complete sacrifice for the child, Cosette. The citizens of the town, such as Madame Victurnien, are pious and moral people who have no conception of the true implication of religious values. They lack charity. Thus, Madeleine stands in sharp contrast: he saves the life of an enemy, and even finds the crippled foe a post as gardener at a convent in Paris. This last fact must be remembered in the later development of the novel. Both Fauchelevent and the charitable act of Madeleine will bear fruit and reward when Jean Valjean is in flight.

Irony and coincidence are also contributing technical devices in this book; these ideas play a major role throughout *Les Misérables*. Fantine believes Jean Valjean to be the cause of all her woes whereas he is her benefactor, and she looks upon Javert as a kind man. The townspeople regard Madeleine as the epitome of a "solid citizen," and he is in fact a social outcast whom they would harass if the truth were known. Coincidence occurs when Fantine "happens" to work in Madeleine's employ; Javert "happens" to be the old guard of the galleys; and Madeleine "happens" to be a witness of the events which lead to Fantine's arrest. There is high drama, even melodrama, in the fifth book: the saving of Fauchelevent; the thrust and counterthrust of the dialogue between Jean Valjean and Javert; and the collapse of Fantine in a faint at the book's end.

Hugo uses exaggeration and hyperbole to win sympathy from the reader, but the plight of Fantine is no doubt very close to a realistic depiction of the miserable condition of the French workers at this time. The author lashes out repeatedly at the society that allowed such sufferings and which sought to grow rich at the expense of fellow human beings. Consequently, there is stirring and contemporary social and moral lesson behind the plot and the ensuing action.

BOOK SIX

Madeleine takes Fantine to his own home, where she is nursed back to health, although it is clear that the years of privation and malnutrition have done her permanent damage. The Thènardiers, who have received a large sum of money from Madeleine, now refuse to give up Cosette so readily because they suppose that the child can be worth a small fortune to them. Madeleine has promised Fantine she will have Cosette with her, and Fantine expects her anxiously. Javert is undergoing "some great interior commotion" and shows "his secret and inveterate aversion for Monsieur Madeleine." At last, another dramatic scene occurs between the foes: Javert demands his own dismissal from the mayor, Madeleine, because he has falsely denounced his superior to higher authorities. Javert has accused Madeleine of being the former convict, Jean Valjean, who robbed a bishop's palace and stole from a small boy! Javert was wrong because a certain Champmathieu has been apprehended as Jean Valjean and will go on trial at Arras the next day. Javert plans to leave that evening to give testimony and return before the trial's end. Madeleine, perturbed that the trial is set so soon, praises Javert instead of firing him; the mayor remains alone in deep thought after Javert's departure. Another crisis is at hand for Jean Valjean.

COMMENT

The themes of pursuit and flight and the conflict over charity versus safety are stressed and amplified in the sixth book. Madeleine has an open confrontation with Javert about his true identity as Jean Valjean; and the police inspector increases his hatred for this individual who defies his rigid set of values. The two men, unable to come to terms on philosophical and moral grounds, transfer their growing antipathy to the personal level.

It is clear at the conclusion of this short section that one or the other must triumph but that the struggle will be long and bitterly waged. Jean Valjean again has to make a decision as he did in the case of Fauchelevent: to help a fellow human being in misery and thus adhere to Bishop Myriel's wisdom or to do nothing and save oneself. Should one become "engagé," or committed in the defense of humanity? Should one seek personal safety first? Despite his melodrama, Hugo probes surely and sharply this conflict of values in his hero, Jean Valjean, and the outcome is not yet certain. In this respect, *Les Misérables* certainly seems to adhere to the path of Realism. Both Javert and Jean Valjean are logically portrayed, and the dialogue is dynamic; indeed, the whole atmosphere is one of high suspense.

Of course, Hugo is still a Romantic: irony is very apparent in the fact that Javert believes himself wrong in his accusations and is in fact quite correct and quite in character in his personality of the implacable detective. Jean Valjean is in the same fashion quite ironic when he insists that Javert should receive promotion instead of dismissal for his investigative prowess. The mayor with his cryptic and laconic comments on Javert's protestations and his keen questions adds immeasurably to the inherent irony of this interview. The actions and reactions of the Thènardiers, vital to bear in mind throughout the novel, and the tragic requests of Fantine for Cosette, are Romantic in emphasizing and contrasting the good and bad, the noble and ignoble qualities of humans.

BOOK SEVEN

Madeleine has decided to save the old former convict, Champmathieu, for he cannot live with his conscience otherwise. In a remarkable section of stream of consciousness and psychological analysis Jean Valjean realizes "that men saw his mask, but the bishop saw his face." He knows too that "there is one spectacle grander than the sky, that is the interior of the soul," and "that the bishop had marked the first phase of his new life, and that this Champmathieu marked the second." He hastens to Arras in secret and hopes at first that his acquaintance in prison may be acquitted. However, when Jean Valjean comprehends that the verdict will send this innocent soul to the galleys for life in his place, he stands up in the courtroom and proves to the astonished audience that he, Madeleine, respected mayor of M____ sur M____, is in reality the wanted prisoner. By references to facts relating to his term in the galleys, Jean Valjean leaves no doubt about his identity. He does not intend in the least to escape and says finally: "I am going, since I am not arrested. I have many things to do. Monsieur the prosecuting attorney knows where I am going, and will have me arrested when he chooses."

COMMENT

This sixth book is dominated by Jean Valjean and brilliantly portrays the agony of his soul. Hugo has skillfully balanced and counter-balanced the forces within his hero's spirit; for instance, Jean Valjean exclaims to the court: "You all, all who are here, think me worthy of pity, do you not? Great God! when I think of what I have been on the point of doing, I think myself worthy of envy. Still, would that all this had not happened!" He is proud of the victory over himself and his definitive embrace of the bishop's idealism, but Jean Valjean would be less than human—and less acceptable in the eyes of the reader—if he had not wished to continue as Madeleine. The descriptions of the courtroom, the officers of the court, the lawyers, witnesses, and viewers offer a sparkling vignette of justice under the Restoration. For example, the mention of Fantine's seducer as a member of the jury adds an ironic note. Hugo is bitter about the perversion of the law into a bulwark of the established classes in society. There is no mercy and no understanding toward the criminal; in fact, the accused is clearly "guilty until proved innocent." Without funds, the poor can but throw themselves at the feet of the judge and jury, as Champmathieu attempts, and the probable result will be rejection of any plea for pity. All the participants of the judicial process are bored and want nothing to disturb the smooth execution of decisions which will preserve the *status quo*. Madeleine's outburst is a severe blow at their class and their values. And they change immediately from respect and flattery toward the mayor into hatred and scorn of the culprit, Jean Valjean.

BOOK EIGHT

Jean Valjean returns to his home and tries to comfort the ailing Fantine with the promise that he will bring Cosette to her. The terrible anguish he has been undergoing is seen by the fact that his hair has turned white overnight. Javert receives orders for Madeleine's arrest and hastens to execute the command in his attitude of "all the evil of good." Another dramatic encounter between Jean Valjean and Javert ensues in the bedroom of Fantine. Javert's terrible revenge in seizing the compliant Jean Valjean, and the police inspector's revelation of his true status, cause Fantine to suffer an immediate relapse. She dies from the shock of the revelation and the loss of hope about recovering Cosette.

Javert's implacable attitude arouses his prisoner to fury, and Valjean approaches the policeman with an iron bar. The pursuer then allows his prisoner a few moments alone with the dead Fantine; afterwards, Jean Valjean docilely follows Javert to the prison. However, he escapes from the cell and goes back to his house. Before he can prepare himself for another flight, Javert enters; and Sister Simplice, "who had never lied in her life," now lies to Javert about the fugitive's presence in the same room. After Javert's exit, Jean Valjean instructs the gentle nun to use the money he is leaving for the trial's cost, expenses of Fantine's funeral, and the rest for the poor. He heads in the direction of Paris.

COMMENT

The whole, delicate structure of Madeleine's (Jean Valjean's) world collapses in this eighth book as a result of his admission of the truth in the courtroom at Arras. A touch of irony is inserted in the reason why the judge decreed Madeleine's arrest: in the course of the mayor's confession, he had said "the Emperor" instead of "Bonaparte." This terminology smacked of evil for a determined royalist such as the judge. The townspeople naturally turn against Madeleine, and the familiar cries of "I told you so" and "I knew it all the time" are heard throughout the area. And of course the rumor that Madeleine was a Bonapartist removes any lingering sentiment of sympathy toward him. Only one person, [Sister Simplice, shows charity, and demonstrates a thesis of Hugo in the novel that goodness can be contagious, and so can evil. A good act is like a stone dropped in water: the ensuing ripples spread beyond the center of the action.]

Unfortunately, Jean Valjean's last intentions as Madeleine are not strictly observed because the village priest, in charge of distributing the funds he left, decides not to waste the money on a convict's expenses and a fallen woman's grave. He keeps the lion's share of the funds for the poor, but Hugo wryly observes that "he did well perhaps."

In this closing book of Part One, Javert and Jean Valjean are now irreconcilable opponents, which action had been increasing in intensity from their first meeting. Fantine disappears from the story, and Cosette will become the leading female character of the novel. Javert will pursue Jean Valjean relentlessly; the capture and imprisonment of this hapless man has become an obsession with him. Jean Valjean, in the eyes of Javert, does not follow the pattern of the criminal; and because of the strange and unusual ways of this individual, Javert's world will likewise crumble if he cannot subdue him. In short, the career of Jean Valjean as Madeleine resembles a circle: he leaves M____ sur M____ in exactly the same way he first appeared, poor, secretly, and unnoticed.

GENERAL COMMENTARY

Three characters dominate the events of Part One: Bishop Myriel, Javert, and Jean Valjean. Although Fantine appears throughout the books of the first part, she is more of a symbol of Hugo's ideas about the victimizing of the poor and the miserable than a fully rounded character. Rather, Fantine symbolizes the condition of the thousands of poor, ignorant young women flocking to the cities for work in the new factories of the Industrial Revolution. She is converted into an image of social injustice, but at the same time, Fantine is the rather typical heroine encountered in Romanticism: doomed by adverse circumstances to perish unremembered and unmoaned, the victim of love and society's callous attitudes. She is the center around which Jean Valjean and Javert struggle.

Bishop Myriel, on the other hand, although a minor character in terms of the number of pages devoted to him in the novel, is one of Victor Hugo's most memorable characters. Like the real person on whom the character is based, the saintly bishop advances the philosophy and idealism of the novelist. Without the bishop, there would be no logical explanation for Jean Valjean's behavior; and without this prelate, the themes of redemption and salvation through love and humanitarianism would be missing in *Les Misérables*.

In addition, *Les Misérables* is also one of the first great detective stories. The ideas of pursuit and flight, as in all the examples of the genre, unfold with repetition and yet with variety. Although the action may enthrall the reader, the underlying philosophies of Jean Valjean and Javert are of the utmost concern in the novel's progress. Both men express the motives of Hugo in the writing of *Les Misérables*, which he explained in a letter to Lamartine, his fellow writer and compatriot in the cause of freedom and liberalism: "Yes, as much as it is permitted man to will, I come to destroy human fate, I condemn slavery, I drive away poverty, I teach ignorance, I treat sickness, I light up the night, I hate hatred. This is what I am, and that is why I wrote *Les Misérables*. To my mind, *Les Misérables* is nothing other than a book having fraternity for a base and progress for a summit." Jean Valjean and Javert are conceived in terms of an antithesis, and as the novel develops, they become increasingly opposed. Antithesis is one of Hugo's favorite stylistic devices throughout the novel, and examples abound. For example, he employs an antithesis for a moral conclusion, as in Jean Valjean's outburst in the court, "After a great crisis, a great trial"; and for the psychological and philosophical explanation of his hero's change in character, "It was more than a transformation—it was a transfiguration." But within the larger frame of reference, the reader must keep his attention focused on Jean Valjean and Javert.

The action of Part One occurs between the years 1815 and 1823, during the Restoration; and Hugo has deliberately made use of this historical period to show his antipathy for the return of the Bourbons. Despite the use of coincidence, the First Part has a clear and logical structure: the degradation of Jean Valjean, the saving grace of the prelate, the initiation of salvation, the struggle for rehabilitation, the challenge to a life of security and ease, the decision to follow Bishop Myriel's admonitions, and the return to exile as a social outcast. Hugo's digressions, which play so prominent a role in *Les Misérables,* are revelatory of the author's thought which is reflected in his whole conception of the novel. For example, in the fifth book, Hugo's ruminations on the importance of animals as creatures of God should make us reflect upon all creation; and in the first book, he declares himself against capital punishment through the feelings of Bishop Myriel and specifically condemns the use of the guillotine. Thus, the digressive excursions of Victor Hugo offer wealth of thought and variety of literary and philosophical speculation. As a consequence, the student should not be discouraged as he starts Part Two to find that the story of Jean Valjean is temporarily abandoned for a long discussion of the Battle of Waterloo.

PART II: COSETTE

BOOK ONE

In the first book of Part II, little action relevant to the plot occurs. Instead, Hugo embarks upon a long and detailed examination of the Battle of Waterloo. However, he inserts one fictitious episode which will have bearing upon the story: Thènardier, the sergeant at Waterloo (about which fact he so ostentatiously bragged in the first book), prowled about the battlefield on the night after the slaughter in search of loot from the corpses. He accidentally helps an important French officer, whom he had intended to strip of valuable objects; and this cavalryman, Pontmercy, promises him lasting gratitude.

COMMENT

The pages of this digression into recent French history are among the most stirring and colorful in the novel even though they are extraneous to the story of Jean Valjean. The Waterloo insertion helps make *Les Misérables* famous as an historical novel. Hugo attacks the Napoleonic legend here, which had so increased in popularity in France that the Corsican's nephew was able to mount the throne as Napoleon III. Therefore, there is a deep political bias in Hugo's critique of the effect of Waterloo: he is really throwing darts at the figure of his enemy, Napoleon III. The novelist studies the excuses for why the French lost the battle: rain the night before which slowed the attack; the unexpected sunken road of Ohain.

In an impassioned critique of Waterloo, Hugo outlines his own concept of history: "Was it possible that Napoleon should win this battle? We answer no. Why? Because of Wellington? Because of Blucher? No. Because of God." According to Hugo, history was moving forward, and in the coming great chain of events of the nineteenth century, Napoleon was an anachronism— he was out of place in the modern age. Thus, for Hugo, "Waterloo is not a battle; it is the change of front of the universe." Here again is the use of antithesis already observed in Part I. Hugo shows himself to be an accurate judge of history in according such decisive weight to Waterloo as the end of the era that had started in 1789 with the French Revolution, and the beginning of a new age in Europe. Destiny, that force that is likewise noted in *Les Misérables* as part and parcel of the lives of the protagonists, is the fulcrum of history; the Infinite exists beyond the power of man to overcome. The terrible losses in manpower evoke in the novelist a humanitarian spirit at the frightful cost of peace in Europe.

BOOK TWO

After the disappearance of Madeleine, the town of M_____ sur M_____ sinks again into poverty without his industrious hands at the helm of business. The newspapers report that Jean Valjean has been apprehended by the authorities and sent back to the galleys. One day, the ship, "Orion", appears in the harbor of Toulon, and the citizens see a thrilling sight. A sailor, having lost his balance, clings precariously to a rope of a sail; he is rescued by a convict who then apparently falls into the sea and is drowned. On the next day. the *Toulon Journal* announces that the name of the missing convict is, of course, Jean Valjean.

COMMENT

Coincidence again comes to Valjean's rescue; the events are explained through a skillful use of third person techniques. The description of the impoverished town after Madeleine's exit depicts a scene typical of the frequent and mysterious depressions that the Industrial Revolution caused to the economies of many hamlets.

BOOK THREE

Cosette has spent almost all her eight years of life with the Thènardiers and has suffered enormously, especially when Fantine stopped sending money for her support. On Christmas eve in 1823, she is sent out in the dark and cold on an errand by the cruel Thènardiers, who seem to out-do each other in inflicting hardships on the child. Their own two daughters, Eponine and Azelma, are spoiled while Cosette is treated worse than a servant. Cosette meets a stranger—Jean Valjean—on the way, and he helps her. He enters the Thènardiers' inn, and they decide to cheat him as much as possible on the bill. When they realize that he is greatly interested in Cosette, the Thènardiers have the idea that luck is now favoring them. Jean Valjean buys Cosette a doll, her first toy, and notices how ugly she is because of neglect. When he submits to all the reckonings of the Thènardiers and settles all bills of Cosette in return for the child, the evil pair at first rejoice. Then, when Jean Valjean and Cosette set out for Paris, the Thènardiers regret not having demanded more money.

With Jean Valjean, Cosette "felt somewhat as if she were near God." When Thènardier pursues Jean Valjean and Cosette in search of money matters—more blackmail—he is astonished to see Fantine's letter of authorization about taking the child. Jean Valjean's detailed information about the past further puzzles him, and he is frightened away. Jean Valjean and Cosette arrive in Paris. He spends money lavishly on her from funds he had laid away before fleeing the town of M＿＿ sur M＿＿.

COMMENT

Good and evil are sharply and dramatically compared and contrasted in the scenes between the Thènardiers and Jean Valjean. The Thènardiers are portrayed as reprehensible, and they gain no sympathy. Likewise, Cosette and the two spoiled daughters of the Thènardiers are presented as opposites. At the same time, it must be remembered that Jean Valjean has created two bitter enemies in the Thènardiers, who will haunt him later. However, the action of Valjean's story now shifts definitely to Paris from the provinces.

BOOK FOUR

Jean Valjean finds shelter for himself and Cosette in an isolated quarter of the city of Paris. Nine months have passed since Fantine's death. He is now fifty-five and Cosette is eight; and he feels that "something new was entering his soul." He has never known love, and Cosette likewise has never enjoyed tenderness. Mutual affection grows between them and they exchange expressions of warmth. However, Jean Valjean notices that one evening the beggar on the street to whom he is accustomed to giving a few coins resembles Javert. On the following evening, the old man again is himself. Jean Valjean thinks it is a question of nerves until he hears a sound in the house one night and sees through the keyhole the figure of Javert. The landlady explains that another gentleman of independent means, such as Jean Valjean, has taken lodgings in the house. As a result of this episode, Jean Valjean and Cosette flee.

COMMENT

This brief book marks the beginning of the love between Jean Valjean and Cosette; the unfortunate man will regard her as the child he never had, and Cosette sees in him a father. The author also stresses the power of love, the sentiment that can overcome the preponderance of politics and war. The initial indications of the growing love between Jean Valjean and Cosette introduce a major idea into the novel that will be followed to the conclusion. Hugo, in describing the house and neighborhood, will probe all the details of the history that has swirled about the residence. He creates deftly and with much (even excessive) detail the background of the story. The appearance of Javert, as will be explained later, is really a coincidence, as the police inspector is on another assignment. But the destiny of Jean Valjean, the Romantic hero, must be fatal; and he cannot rest in his wanderings.

BOOK FIVE

This book is one of the most suspenseful in the entire novel as Javert reappears and resumes the chase. Javert had made a serious investigation of the Jean Valjean case and was satisfied his foe had been killed in the harbor of Toulon. Even the Thènardiers' story about the stranger who took a child with him, which Javert had read in the newspapers, did not change his opinion about Valjean's demise. However, Javert was just as astonished as Jean Valjean when the two recognized each other on the street corner. Javert had disguised himself only for one evening as the beggar. Then, Javert went on the hunt in earnest, renting a room near that of Jean Valjean.

Hugo lovingly describes the streets, houses, and bridges of Paris as Jean Valjean flees with Cosette from Javert and the other police. However, Valjean is eventually trapped by his lack of knowledge of the city and finds himself in a blind alley with no way out. Then, as he hears faint sounds of chanting nearby, he scales a wall into a garden and eludes his pursuers. Inside a building on the property, Jean Valjean and Cosette encounter Fauchelevent. The old man recognizes his benefactor, Madeleine, and shelters them in this convent of the Petit Picpus. Javert, unable to fathom how his prey has eluded the trap, returns crestfallen to the Prefecture of Police.

COMMENT

Here, of course, is a flagrant use of coincidence to solve the plot situation, but the reader should be prepared to forgive Hugo for his stretch of the imagination, because other coincidences are to come in the novel. The Romantic convention works: the action is so dramatic and the sympathy of the audience is so much on Valjean's side at this point that anything can be allowed to rescue the hero. Hugo knows how to tell a story and capture his reader's imagination; the details of Paris are so realistic that they compensate for the use of coincidence.

Likewise, the reappearance of Fauchelevent illustrates one of the outstanding lessons of *Les Misérables:* charity rebounds to the giver, and good works are repaid in kind. Hugo is forcefully attempting to sway French public opinion to the ideals of humanitarianism and kindness; and he is appealing to the basic instincts of his readers by showing that all men will profit from idealism. Jean Valjean has now made another fateful decision: he will devote the rest of his life to Cosette; in return, "he should need nothing except for her, and fear nothing save on her account." A touch of Romantic irony comes in Fauchelevent's total dedication to Valjean's ideals; and the old gardener gently berates the former Madeleine for forgetting the debt due him. The converted enemy is clearly a friend and ally, and Fauchelevent has tried to live like this toward all men since the days at M___ sur M___.

Javert has suffered another defeat, which has only served to intensify his rage at Valjean's elusive nature. Despite his bad luck and some blunders, Javert is the model of the modern detective—or as Hugo states, "he was none the less one of the wisest and most correct detectives that ever existed." A psychological aspect to this quest is beginning to dominate all Javert's thoughts: the freedom of Jean Valjean symbolizes the destruction of all law, order, and authority. And this man at liberty is the defeat of his life's dedication to these pillars of the social system.

BOOK SIX

No action occurs in this very short book; in fact, none of the characters appears throughout the pages of the section. However, the reader is given a detailed explanation of the convent of No. 62 Petite Rue Picpus, which will be home to Jean Valjean and Cosette for a long period. The author emphasizes the history and traditions of the religious order, the background of some of the nuns residing there now, and the life within the cloistered house. It is important to note that this residence is the home of nuns who do not go into the world but who remain totally isolated from the activities of daily life. For Jean Valjean, the condition of his sanctuary is beyond all expectations: no one enters this convent without permission, and the residents go out only with great difficulty.

COMMENT

These descriptions of the cloistered life of nuns were controversial in Hugo's day, because he was trying to explain the role of such a system in a modern society. Although anticlerical and unappreciative of the spiritual values of such an existence, Hugo still tries to be impartial, and he writes that "we do not comprehend everything, but we insult nothing." In general, nevertheless, Hugo does not favor such a life for the nineteenth century; he feels strongly that it is against human nature, reason, and the rule of civilization. But as a child of the Enlightenment, he avoids extremism and concludes this digressive sixth book with these words: "As to convents, they present a complex question. A question of civilization, which condemns them; a question of liberty, which protects them." It is worthwhile to notice that the author balances his ideas by means of the favorite antithesis, so common throughout the novel.

Hugo foresees sharply and accurately the problems of his age; and indeed, one of the preponderant merits of *Les Misérables,* which has contributed to its continuing popularity, is the insight it provides into the past century. Thus, Hugo summarizes the religious dilemma: "In the nineteenth century the religious idea is undergoing a crisis." But the author is prepared with a substitute set of values and urges consideration of new ideals when he continues that "we are unlearning certain things, and we do well, provided that while unlearning one thing we are learning another. No vacuum in the human heart!" Here is a concise and conclusive summary of Hugo's idealism: if religion does not provide an answer to the crisis of the human soul—and remember that the good Bishop Myriel was an example of the nobility of religious virtues—then other ideals must be found for the crisis of the nineteenth century. In *Les Misérables* Hugo is drawing a sketch of a society devoid of all true faith and idealism. As a consequence, these digressions, slowing down the pace of the novel, offer fascinating and stimulating glimpses of the world of Victor Hugo.

BOOK SEVEN

Hugo continues with his digressions but broadens his vision to a consideration of the Unknown and the Infinite as he defines God. Although the monastic life embraces the concept of withdrawal to arrive at God, Hugo does not admit that this manner of life and prayer is the correct course of conduct. No action takes place in this book, and none of the characters has a part in it.

COMMENT

Hugo perhaps expresses his hopes for humanity in the apparently contradictory but significant phrase: "We are for religion against the religions." He is unable to adhere to any dogmatic or theological basis in his belief in God, and even avoids the word in favor of the vaguer terms, Unknown and Infinite. His belief in the individual man also precludes any adherence to a fixed formula of worship. It is well to bear in mind that this attitude of the author is very Romantic: the stress upon the single person, the emphasis upon freedom and liberty, and the revolt against control and authority. If man follows these principles in his desire to encounter God, he will meet the Unknown or the Infinite in his soul and in his behavior; and as a result, Hugo states: "The Unknown is an ocean. What is conscience? It is the compass of the Unknown." The sixth and seventh books of Part II have to be read together; here, the logical progression of Hugo's spirit toward belief in some form, however nebulous it may seem, of an eternal verity, comes to light.

Hugo's fundamental philosophy, however, has deep roots in the Age of Reason and Romanticism; he concentrates his vision on the individual and on that individual's rights in a republican society. His prophetic defense of this comparatively new and untried system of government and way of life is as a continuation of any true and lasting religious ideals. Thus, he digresses in antithetical style: "The grandeur of democracy is that it denies nothing and renounces nothing of humanity. Close by the rights of Man, side by side with them, at least, are the rights of the Soul." When the reader considers that these striking statements were written more than one hundred years ago, before 1862, Hugo's power and popularity should be appreciated. Likewise, it is necessary to grasp the importance of not omitting the many diversionary exercises in philosophy, religious thought, and political doctrine in the novel. The narrative may suffer and the action be halted completely in these two books, but Hugo's fascinating mind and provocative ideas cannot be dismissed. Without these brilliant outpourings of the author's mind, *Les Misérables* would not be the great work it is.

BOOK EIGHT

Although Fauchelevent is determined to repay Madeleine for the kindness of the past, problems exist about providing shelter for the former mayor and the little girl. For one thing, Fauchelevent faces the issue of explaining the presence of the two in the cloistered convent. However, chance again intervenes: the bells of the convent announce the death of an aged and pious nun, Mother Crucifixion; and Fauchelevent sees in the resultant activity of the sisters the occasion to smuggle Cosette out of the property in a basket. At the same time, Mother Innocent, the prioress, summons Fauchelevent to explain that the dead sister is not to be buried outside the convent but inside the chapel. This action is to be concealed from the authorities; and Fauchelevent, taking advantage of the embarrassed posture of the prioress, insists that he will require the aid of his brother. After some hesitation, his request is granted; in this way Fauchelevent's "brother" and his "brother's grandchild" will be able to come to the convent and consequently reside there.

First, however, some rather dramatic episodes ensue: Jean Valjean must be smuggled out in the supposed coffin of Mother Crucifixion. Fauchelevent has the plan to meet the usual fellow gravedigger Mestienne, put the coffin into the ground, and then as usual invite Mestienne for some drinks before they start to pile the dirt on top of the coffin. Thus Jean Valjean will be able to escape from the coffin in the interval. But a disconcerting and almost fatal surprise awaits Fauchelevent: Mestienne has died, and the new grave-digger is a serious fellow who wants to complete the work first. In fact, Jean Valjean faints from lack of air as the dirt is piled on top of the coffin until Fauchelevent turns pickpocket, takes the work permit of the new helper, and sends the man home for the card. Finally, Jean Valjean is liberated and revived; Cosette and he now enter the convent area formally, and a new existence begins.

COMMENT

Despite the necessity to change dwelling places from fear of Javert and the authorities, Jean Valjean is happier at the conclusion of this book than at any time in the past. He now has Cosette with him, and he has found a place of refuge. Of course, this eighth book exhibits Hugo's anticlericalism in his biting descriptions of the way of life of the nuns, and most specifically, their dedication to an unsanitary and unwholesome manner of existence in the burial rites of Mother Crucifixion. Hugo believes in progress and a beneficent materialism as worthy ideas to be adopted for civilized people. Thus he attacks the archaic procedures of Mother Innocent. When established religion is at variance with civil and modern concepts, then the former can expect no sympathy from Hugo. The departure, close brush with death, and entrance again into the cloister are skillfully drawn with a sure hand of the artist. If luck and coincidence can play to advantage in the travails of Jean Valjean, so also can these forces work to his disadvantage.

To any charge of overemphasis in favor of his hero's escapades, Hugo can answer effectively that these powers over the human fortunes are beyond human control. Human beings experience both good and bad luck; all in all, Hugo has balanced the qualities well throughout the novel. Perhaps one may carp at the excessive use of this technical device, but there can be no complaint that the novelist has not tried to effect a compromise in the woes and windfalls that beset his protagonist. The scene between the gravediggers, with the unfortunate Jean Valjean close to death from suffocation, exploits all the varied possibilities of Romantic irony. On the surface, it is rather amusing: the pleadings of Fauchelevent, and the obdurate devotion to duty of the new gravedigger. Once Hugo has extracted all dramatic interest and ironic humor from the scene and rescued the hero, he concludes the book quite rapidly with a happy vignette of the two reunited in the convent thanks to Fauchelevent's improvisations. In fact, the future existence of the fugitives is already indicated as isolated but safe.

GENERAL COMMENTARY

The time encompassed by the second part of *Les Misérables* is more compressed than in the first part; all the events occur between 1823 and 1824. But the episodes are obviously a continuation of the narrative line set in motion beforehand. There are four outstanding facets of the plot that take place in Book Two: the return of Jean Valjean from another imprisonment in the galleys; the journey to the Thènardiers as a result of which he rescues Cosette; the discovery by Javert, pursuit, and escape from the relentless police inspector; and the fortunate shelter of the cloister. Javert and the Thènardiers, who will continue to play major roles in the lives of Jean Valjean and Cosette, hold the plot together by their fortuitous appearances at crucial moments. Although digressions may delay the story of Jean Valjean, the novel shows the sure and able hand of a master craftsman in the construction of Books One and Two. By no means do the digressions betray a careless writer because *Les Misérables* shows a definite and mature structure. There is unity and parallelism between the "Fantine" and "Cosette" divisions— the names themselves indicate that the novelist wanted this facet to be quite apparent to the reader and to the critic.

In both parts, Jean Valjean is rejected by society and is at the point of being seized by the police; and in both parts, he is rescued by "two houses of God," as Hugo depicts the situation at the end of Part II. Bishop Myriel set Jean Valjean on the path of righteousness, and without this example of charity, Valjean would have relapsed into crime. The sanctuary which Jean Valjean secured in the convent prevented his seizure by Javert for punishment in the galleys. However, Hugo has advanced beyond this evident and planned structural concept to insert a new virtue into the theme of charity and redemption: love. Love enters the life of Jean Valjean for the first time, and he dedicates his whole existence to Cosette; in return, he is happier than he has ever been. Indeed, the second part of *Les Misérables* terminates on an unmistakably happy and optimistic note; the outcast and fugitive has perhaps eluded his pursuers and has mastered an adverse fate.

The digressions in this part illuminate two major concerns of Hugo: history and religion. Some critics have argued that the narration of Waterloo is in the highest tradition of the historical novel; and although there may be some inaccuracies in the light of more recent historical research about the facts of the battle, Hugo's account nevertheless makes the engagement come alive. He employs facts and details in a highly dramatic sense and tries to interpret the military movements in terms of the human beings involved. But beyond Hugo's narrative and dramatic skill is the profound philosophical outlook he conveys to Waterloo. There is consequently a strong sense of the ideological importance of the battle in the history of the nineteenth century. History does not exist as facts; rather, the facts of history serve as an interpretative guide to the implications of great events. For example, Hugo insists that the cause for Napoleon's defeat was God, by which he means fate or destiny. The Unknown or the Infinite had other plans for the new century, and Hugo, being a good Romantic, expressed much concern with the control over life which chance and coincidence enjoyed. For this reason, in addition to the stylistic and technical problems of organizing the novel, Hugo relied heavily on these two aspects in the development of his hero's life and those around him.

Hugo's religious views or philosophical orientations, the second principal subject of the digressive passages, are closely linked with his concept of history. He has little faith in organized religion and feels that it is an anachronism in the modern world of the nineteenth century. However, Hugo has a strong religious sense; and he expounds a faith in the power of the Infinite or the Unknown. But the religious values are not theological or metaphysical; and on the contrary, people should occupy themselves with the contemporary arena of earthly activity. True spiritual traits are revealed in the actions of humanity; and most especially, in the themes of humanitarianism, charity, and love. From the faith of a past age, Hugo is groping for a new faith: a faith in God's creatures or the human beings under the power of the Infinite and the Unknown. This is another cause for Hugo's inquiry into the "personality of God" in this Part II of *Les Misérables*.

In short, although the action of Part II is less dynamic than it might be, the "Cosette" section of the novel is rich in digressions that add to Hugo's stature and to the comprehension of his spirit. The danger of abridged and edited versions of *Les Misérables* lies in the possible exclusion of these revelatory passages; without the digressions, the novel would not be the panorama of nineteenth-century France which it is. Thus, the reader should not be discouraged by the length of a particular part and the seemingly rambling manner of discussion.

PART III: MARIUS

BOOK ONE
A lengthy description of Paris and the fate of the *gamin,* or
street urchin, is inserted at the beginning of this book. One
gamin in particular is singled out as representative: Gavroche Jondrette. Gavroche lives with his father, mother, and
two sisters in the house where Jean Valjean first lived in
with Cosette after coming to Paris. Next to the Jondrette
family lives a very poor young man, Marius.

COMMENT
There is apparently no connection between these new
characters and the persons already playing their roles
in the novel—and the plot. However, the Jondrettes
are really the Thènardiers in new guise. The fact that
the building is the same one that Jean Valjean used as
a hiding place will be of more than passing interest.
Marius will be of increasing interest to Cosette, for he
will become her lover; and even the Thènardiers—or
Jondrettes—will be linked by fate to Marius. All these
explanations come afterwards, but readers will comprehend Hugo's purposes to better advantage if they
are informed at the outset about the true situation. Little by little, the astute novelist will unravel and tie up
anew the strands of supposedly unconnected threads.
In the lively narrative on Paris and the *gamins,* Hugo
exposes his love, knowledge, and sympathy for the
capital and these outcasts. He uses a metaphor to sum
up his impressions: "The *gamin* is the expression of
Paris, and Paris is the expression of the world." Hugo
has overwhelming confidence in these underdogs of
society and philosophizes that one may "look through
the medium of the people, and you shall discern the
truth."

BOOK TWO

Here is a portrait of a royalist of the eighteenth century, according to Hugo. Luke Esprit Gillenormand is ninety years old and is cared for by his daughter, Mademoiselle Gillenormand the elder. The younger daughter married "the man of her dreams," but she is now dead. The grandson of this marriage lives with the two Gillenormands.

COMMENT

The reader is still unaware of the relationship of all these new characters to the story of Jean Valjean. The explanation will come later: Marius is the child of the marriage between Gillenormand's daughter and a French officer, Pontmercy. Nevertheless, the background of the old monarchist is interesting because it provides an example of the conservative and middle-class support for the king. Gillenormand is a fascinating portrait of the stuffy bourgeois who helped provoke the French Revolution by his ignorance of the miserable plight of the peasants and his blind loyalty to the trappings of the Bourbons. In the nineteenth century, he is an amusing anachronism who is at the same time dangerous because he tries to block change and the desires of youth to express itself. Despite the social and political meanings in the person of Gillenormand, Hugo knows how to draw a realistic sketch of a character for his novel; and the stubborn monarchist comes vividly to life.

BOOK THREE

Marius is brought up as a royalist and is introduced in only the most conservative salons of Restoration society. He has grown up with little knowledge of his father, George Pontmercy, a brave officer in the armies of Napoleon I and a vehement defender of the Bonapartist cause. Thus the marriage of an obdurate royalist's daughter to an enemy of everything which old Gillenormand advocated was a terrible blow to the old man. With the collapse of the Napoleonic Empire in 1815, Pontmercy is penniless; and the death of his wife that same year caused him to make a hard decision. He turned over Marius to Gillenormand so that the boy could have the advantages of a home and the promise of a legacy in the future. The Gillenormands have felt no remorse at the manner in which they have sought to eradicate Marius's memory of his father. However, in 1827, Marius is sent by his grandfather to see his father, who is dying. As a result of his hurried trip, Marius—who arrives shortly after his father has died—becomes devoted to the memory of Colonel Pontmercy and to that of his cause, Bonapartism.

Although this hero of Waterloo has left practically no material objects of value, he has bequeathed in a note to his son the title of baron received on the battlefield from Napoleon; and the obligation to help at any cost a sergeant Thènardier who rescued him. Marius is enamored of the "Napoleon Legend," and the Gillenormands suspect only that he is in love with some girl. A cousin, Lieutenant Théodule Gillenormand, is commissioned by them to follow Marius and find out about his mysterious trips; the young officer, disconcerted to find that Marius pays visits to the grave of Colonel Baron Pontmercy, keeps silent. However, the Gillenormands accidentally find a number of calling cards which Marius has had printed as Baron Marius Pontmercy; and they also come upon the note from the late colonel telling about the title.

After Napoleon's fall, the Restoration had denied any title to Pontmercy because of his association with the emperor. In a bitter scene with the Gillenormands, Marius proclaims his loyalty to the cause of his father and shocks his relatives with the expression: "Down with the Bourbons, and the great hog Louis XVIII!" Marius is dismissed from the house, but he is granted a monthly allowance by his royalist grandfather. Sorrowful because of his deep love for the young man, old Gillenormand nevertheless orders his name never to be mentioned in the house again.

COMMENT

The story is advanced in this book by the explanation of the background of Marius; and the name of Thènardier, so pervasive throughout the novel, again appears in the limelight. The reader is certainly prepared psychologically for some connection between this rogue and the hero, Jean Valjean. However, there is still no clue as to how the author will tie up these loose ends and bring his characters together. Hugo's Romantic ideas unfold in the book through the employment of sentimentality; nobility of personality; the rebellion, enthusiasm, and idealism of youth; and the frank appeal to the emotions. For example, Marius enters the deathroom of his father and gazes at the face of the colonel, on which a big tear had fallen; "this tear was for his son's delay," as Hugo comments. Marius is a symbol of the Romantic who fought the literary and political battles of Hugo's own youth.

The novelist is also trying to analyze and dissect the attraction of the "Napoleon Legend" after his death in exile at St. Helena. After all, his sworn enemy, Napoleon III, had risen to power on the reputation and memory of his ancestor rather than on his own rather meager merits. The Restoration provided stability and order for the older generation but created no spark of interest and ardor in the young generation. This age group had never known the sufferings and casualties of the Napoleonic Era and thus looked "romantically" upon an age which offered ideals and glory. Although the sympathies of Hugo are with Marius in the novel, the author is really more concerned about the phenomenon of the messianic name of Napoleon over his generation. Here is the preparation for the riots and rebellions that are depicted later in the novel; and here likewise are the antithetical forces of youth versus old age, the new against the old, and the Restoration facing the demands of the people.

BOOK FOUR

Marius leads a precarious but stimulating life in Paris. His standard of living declines steadily but his pride is steadfast; for example, he refuses the allowance granted him by old Gillenormand. His attempts to earn a livelihood are not very profitable, but he continues to strive for independence. Marius joins a political club, The Friends of the ABC, and becomes more committed than ever to the ideals of his father. From adulation of Napoleon, he progresses to study of the French Revolution. Progress is the magic word for these young men; and Marius is among the leading voices against the Restoration.

COMMENT

This short book traces the political development of Marius—and indirectly the youth of the Restoration—for the ground swell that would lead to the overthrow of the reactionary regime; and for the democratic and liberal struggle of the century in France. Hugo observes wryly and indirectly that these eager souls are sincere and idealistic, but that they lack a shrewd political sense. For example, they are very disunited in their goals and in their plans for obtaining great changes and reforms. Instead of presenting dry facts, the novelist dissects the heart of the revolutionary movement in the nineteenth century; he sketches the positive and negative attitudes of the potential rebels. None of them belongs to the proletariat for which they intend to fight; they are all members of the established classes who should have been content with their station in life. However, they are prepared for sacrifices to work for republicanism. Actually, Hugo's heart is completely with these bold individualists.

BOOK FIVE

Marius finally is admitted to the bar and informs his grandfather of this fact by letter. The old man, stubborn and proud, cannot bring himself to answer the letter, but it is clear that he deeply loves Marius. However, Marius at the age of twenty is in no better financial situation; in fact, he has to make increasing sacrifices to live. He abandons temporarily his interest in politics; and except for two friends, Courfeyrac, a young rebel, and Mabeuf, an open-hearted old man, Marius lives a withdrawn life. The isolation and cheapness of the Gorbeau house brings Jean Valjean to this place in 1831. His neighbors are the Jondrettes—alias the Thènardiers—and one day Marius, from his small cash reserve, pays their rent when they are on the verge of being evicted. However, the Jondrettes know nothing of this act of charity. Meanwhile, Aunt Gillenormand, hurt by Marius's refusal to accept any money and by his lack of conciliatory moves, begins to press the advantages of his cousin, Lieutenant Théodule, with the grandfather. Although the officer flatters the old man with defense of the royalist cause, Gillenormand obviously yearns for Marius. For instance, he looks the lieutenant straight in the eyes and one day says: "You are a fool."

COMMENT

Hugo is starting to bring the various threads of his plot together: Marius is in the former house of Jean Valjean, and his life is becoming entwined with the shady path of the Thénardiers. The human problem of alienation between two generations is further exploited in the feelings of Marius and old Gillenormand. Each loves the other, but both are obdurate and will not make the first gesture of peace. Marius is striving to formulate a philosophy of life and is starting to enjoy the sights of

Paris. These pages have the quality slow motion, but Hugo is steadily leading the reader toward an impending confrontation of the characters.

BOOK SIX

Marius, starting to take walks in the large park of the Luxembourg, notices an old man and a young girl together there each day at the same time. As the reader may quickly guess and will learn later, the two are Jean Valjean and Cosette. At first, Marius is favorably impressed by the natural dignity of the man but is rather repelled by the ugliness of the girl. After a time, Marius stops going to the park for about six months; when he resumes the walks, he is surprised to notice how the young lady has changed. She has blossomed into a beautiful flower for the love-struck Marius.

Marius goes now with anticipation to the Luxembourg, dresses more fashionably, and strives with no success to discover her name. A dropped handkerchief with the letters U. F. is really no clue because Marius thinks that the girl's name is "Ursula." Jean Valjean worries about the youth's presence in the park and his interest in them; Marius, anxious to make Cosette's acquaintance, follows the couple to their home. But when he returns to the Luxembourg, they no longer come, and his inquiries at the house reveal that they have moved suddenly.

COMMENT

The story begins to pick up speed and more interest for the reader as the three main characters, Jean Valjean, Marius, and Cosette, find their lives influenced by each other. A variation in the theme of the chase, sentimental and emotional rather than thrilling and suspenseful (as in the case of Jean Valjean and Javert), appears in Marius's frustrated efforts to make the acquaintance of Cosette. In this book, Hugo develops the idea of a young man in love and a girl's coy reactions to a potential suitor; the feelings of the human heart are delicately and accurately probed. This book serves likewise as a light, mildly humorous relief to the high drama of the preceding books—and to the actions that will soon occur.

BOOK SEVEN

A quartet of gangsters rules the underworld of Paris from 1830 until 1835. They work closely together and terrorize the shady environment of their territory; in short, they are the personification of evil. Although there are no sure indications within this book of their connection to the story and to the lives of the main characters, the reader will recognize Hugo's technique of presenting new faces first and later bringing them into focus.

COMMENT

This book—only seven pages long—is an example of Hugo's weakness as a novelist. He fails to provide any clues to his audience about the importance of the *Patron-Minette* gang to the novel's total framework. There are redeeming features for Hugo's technical weakness: the description of the criminal world of the French capital; the psychological analysis of the mind of the man devoted to wickedness; and the typical Hugo philosophical commentary on the problem of evil in the world. He is still an optimist, and he firmly believes in the redemption of these lower types of society. He writes that "Humanity is identity. All men are the same clay. No difference, here below at least, in predestination. The same darkness before, the same flesh during, the same ashes after life. But ignorance, mixed with the human composition, blackens it. This incurable ignorance possesses the heart of man, and there becomes Evil." One may severely castigate Hugo for his failure in the technique of composition; but one must certainly admire the depth of his thought, his humanitarian and charitable gaze, and the lyrical, poetical manner in which he expresses himself.

BOOK EIGHT

Marius has now been living in poverty for five years. In addition to the hardships of his miserable circumstances, he has not been able to see Cosette and Jean Valjean for six months. All his enthusiasm and ardor have vanished; his mood is one of complete depression. One day he thinks that he recognizes Cosette's father dressed as a poor laborer but dismisses the episode as only a resemblance. Of course the worker was Jean Valjean. In the midst of his melancholy, Marius accidentally picks up a packet of letters, all in the same handwriting but addressed to different persons, which contain pleas for money. Shortly thereafter, one of the Jondrette girls, his neighbors next door, gives him furtively a letter from her father in which Thénardier, alias Jondrette, thanks Marius for paying the rent and wants more funds. Marius recognizes the handwriting as the same as that in the four letters already noted; and the young man realizes that his fellow tenants are operating a racket to fleece kind people. After observing the pitiful girl and the misery of the Jondrettes, Marius suddenly comprehends how fortunate he is in his own situation. He thinks himself selfish for so much concentration upon his problems; he should study the rest of humanity more.

Afterwards Marius spies upon the Jondrettes through a hole in the thin wall separating the two apartments and sees more proofs of the abject privation in which they exist. The husband and wife are very unkempt, and the apartment is unclean; the second daughter resembles both parents and the sister in her poor and untidy appearance. At that moment, the daughter who previously came to Marius enters with happy news: an old man and his daughter who have promised to aid them are on the way. When the philanthropist and the girl come into the Jondrette quarters, Marius is stunned: the young woman is the still unknown Cosette—his vanished love—and the gentleman is of course Jean Valjean. Even more astonished or certainly as much so as Marius is Thénardier because he remembers the face of his new benefactor as that of Jean Valjean.

Jean Valjean, having arrived without much money, agrees to return at six o'clock that evening with financial help for the Thénardiers. Marius frantically pursues Jean Valjean and Cosette but has no money with him to pay for a carriage; he notices outside the apartment house that Thénardier is whispering mysteriously with some disreputable looking men—the gang of *Patron-Minette*. Going up the stairs, he meets the Thénardiers' elder daughter and entrusts her with the task of discovering Cosette's address. Marius, resuming his eavesdropping, hears Thénardier tell his wife that their visitor is truly their mortal enemy and that their revenge is at hand. Marius obviously does not know the entire story nor is he aware of the plans in their details against Jean Valjean. However, he is determined to thwart the Thénardiers and protect his beloved's supposed father.

Marius takes the logical course: he goes to the nearest police station and explains all he knows to the police inspector—Javert. Javert senses that the infamous *Patron-Minette* thugs are involved in the plot and also the Thénardiers, who have a bad reputation. Marius is elated that he can help rescue Jean Valjean and Cosette—with the help of Javert—and thus become acquainted with the girl. Marius is to fire one shot into the air at the moment he judges during his spying through the hole in the ceiling that the police should attack. As evening falls, Marius takes his place where he can see into the Jondrette apartment; and they, having sent the older daughter to check his room, believe Marius to be out. Jean Valjean comes to see Thénardier, apparently not recognizing his old foe; however, he is increasingly suspicious as the members of the gang, indicated as poor and deserving neighbors by Thénardier, take their places in the small quarters. At last, Thénardier springs the trap: he confronts Jean Valjean with the past, the rescue of Cosette (who has not accompanied Jean Valjean on this second trip), and the subsequent misfortunes of the Thénardiers which they attribute, in a strange use of logic, to the loss of Cosette. Jean Valjean denies all the accusations of Thénardier, infuriating the wicked man to more outbursts; for example, Thénardier brags that he has been a brave French soldier, fought at Waterloo, and even rescued an important officer, Pontmercy.

Marius is astonished at the news he has just heard: Jondrette is really Thénardier about whom his father has commented: "A man named Thénardier saved my life. If my son should meet him, he will do him all the good he can." And yet, Thénardier is obviously a criminal who should be brought to justice—and who is presently threatening the person whom Marius respects as the father of Cosette, the love of his life. Duty and love begin to struggle in his tormented mind as he listens to the brutal threats of Thénardier. Marius has his hand on the pistol, ready to fire, but cannot make up his mind. Upstairs, Jean Valjean makes a break to escape out the window; after a fierce struggle, he is subdued. Thénardier makes an astute observation that will help him to blackmail Jean Valjean: the latter has never shouted during the whole episode, which signifies to Thénardier that he did not want the police to arrive. Jean Valjean is wanted by the authorities, concludes Thénardier. Thus, Jean Valjean is forced to write a note to Cosette telling her to come to the Thénardier apartment. When Cosette is in their power, Jean Valjean will be released and will bring a large sum of money for her ransom. However, Cosette's address is wrong, and the infuriated ruffians want to kill Jean Valjean, who has succeeded in untying himself in the interval.

A fight to the death ensues: Jean Valjean's strength and advantageous position put the criminals on the defensive. Marius, unable to come to a decision about firing the warning shot, sees nearby the note written by the older of the Thénardier girls that "The cops are here." He tosses this paper into the room; the gang believes that the Thénardier girl just tossed it in through the window; and prepare to escape. At that exact moment, Javert, suspicious that something is amiss with Marius, bursts into the room and apprehends the Thénardiers with their accomplices. For Javert, it is a prize catch; but he is somewhat mystified why the victim of the plotters took advantage of the confusion to jump out the window and disappear. On the next day, the gamin of the first pages of Part III, Gavroche, comes along to see his parents and sisters—the Thénardiers—and is not particularly unhappy to be told they are in jail.

COMMENT

In this very lengthy, final book of Part III, Hugo brings all his main characters from the previous parts together, and he also compounds the sum by adding the new figures who have dominated the part or have been introduced in this third part. For example, the third part is entitled "Marius," and Marius controls much of the action in this last book. The element of melodrama is emphasized throughout book Eight: Will Marius fire the shot? Will Jean Valjean escape from the Thénardiers? And will Javert recognize and capture the elusive opponent? In order to achieve so much suspense and conflict, Hugo has had to strain the technical qualities of coincidence and luck to the utmost. In fact, there is clearly too much reliance upon these forces in the book; but the reader is perhaps not too attentive to the defects in the first reading. He is too mindful of the answers to the important questions posed above. Hugo knows how to hold his audience's attention; and he wants to tell a good story. In this aim, he has obviously achieved a high mark.

The dynamic encounter in the apartment of the Thénardiers is matched by the mental agony of Marius below them; and the lengthening shadow of Javert, appearing only briefly, can destroy the lives of all involved. The dilemma of Marius follows the patterns of French Classical drama, that of Corneille and Racine, in which the protagonists are torn tragically between love and duty. Instead of resolving the problem forcefully, Hugo has relied upon one of his weakest uses of coincidence: the discovery and insertion of the letter into the den of the criminals. As far as Marius's hopes are concerned, he is no better off than at the beginning of the eighth book. He is no closer to knowing Cosette; and he has lost track again of Jean Valjean. On the contrary, he has seen one of his ideals vanish in the light of cold reality: the fact that Thénardier, the supposed savior of his father, is nothing more than a base outlaw and criminal.

GENERAL COMMENTARY

Despite the technical flaws of *Les Misérables,* particularly noticeable in the eighth book of this Part III, there is an overall structural unity within the third section. For example, Gavroche entered the scene in Book One, and reappears at the close of Part III. He connects the story by a humorous thread and perhaps symbolizes the fall of the Thénardiers. Part III is certainly well named—Marius—because the young man is the principal person in almost all the books and is in the middle of all the action. At first glance, the absence of Jean Valjean and Cosette from Part III may strike readers as a defect, but these characters were living in the convent and enjoying the anonymity which Jean Valjean wanted so desperately. There would have been little point to describing their prosaic existence since the author had already dedicated so much space in Part II to the background of the cloister.

Marius is introduced in 1827, and the third part ends probably in late 1831. Thus, Hugo is now compressing the time span of his novel. This maneuver will be intensified in the last two parts of *Les Misérables*. Marius' family, particularly his father and grandfather, receive much attention because the two men symbolize two violently opposed ideals, the French Revolution and the Napoleonic Era, and the Restoration of the Bourbon Monarchy in 1815. Marius' conversion to revolutionary ideas is plausible and represents the problem which the youth of France faced.

One great event is curiously missing from Part III: the Revolution of 1830, which saw the collapse of the Bourbons and the rise of the July Monarchy. In fact, there is scant mention of this fact in Part III, and no impact of this major political change is noted in Marius, old Gillenormand, and the others. Marius and Cosette meet in the summer of 1831, almost in the exact middle of Part III, and this encounter alters radically the course of the plot. Prior to this guarded approach of the two young people, the main focus was on Jean Valjean and his efforts to elude Javert. The love story assumes increasing importance, and the two plots are inextricably linked in the scene at the Thénardiers. The happenings on that wild evening are still narrated in great measure from Marius' point of view; and Jean Valjean and his adversary, Javert, never take center stage. Marius suffers the anguish of having to decide between love and duty; the reader may guess at Jean Valjean's agony at Thénardier's shocking revelation, but he is not provided any introspective passages from the old man's thought. However, when Javert belatedly apprehends the criminals, Marius vanishes from sight; and the reader does not know at the conclusion what has happened to him.

Now that the two main threads of the story, the love theme and the chase idea, have come together, all the characters will find their hopes and fears influenced by each other. In this centralized plot, three principal characters remain: Jean Valjean, Cosette, and Marius. Javert, despite the tremendous power which he wields on the fates of all involved, does not occupy a prominent place.

Hugo is considerably less expansive in his philosophical moods in Part III, and many of the digressive sections deal with Paris and the life of the French capital. The minor characters, such as the Gillenormands, are from the middle classes; the young rebels of the Restoration, as in the political club which Marius joined; and also the lower and debased classes, as in the gangland accomplices of the Thénardiers. Despite the abundance of coincidence and chance to resolve the plot situations, Hugo has an abiding philosophy behind his novelistic technique: he wishes to show that kindness and love win merit for the doer. Charity has brought Marius into contact with the Thénardiers; the same attribute has brought Jean Valjean into a new adventure. On the surface, the results may appear unpleasant, but the reader will see in the coming parts how Victor Hugo proves his theories and beliefs.

PART IV: ST. DENIS

BOOK ONE

The author traces the historical background between 1830 and 1832. The Bourbons fell in 1830, and Louis-Philippe reigns as a bourgeois monarch in the July Monarchy. However, the people are far from satisfied; by the middle of 1832, they are ready for an insurrection. Marius' political club is very active in the planned revolt, but they are annoyed by their friend's obvious distraction and consequent lack of dependability.

COMMENT

Hugo returns to a long digression on his philosophy of history. The Bourbons, unable to adapt themselves to a changing world, have attempted to oppose the nineteenth century; therefore, they have had to vanish from power. Some progress was achieved under them, but not enough; their departure was at least dignified and peaceful. However, the new monarchy has failed to live up to the expectations of the people. Hugo makes many wry and profound comments on human nature and politics as when he writes: "As soon as the revolution strikes the shore, the able carve up the wreck." The novelist blames the bourgeoisie for the failure of the revolution; this middle class has secured its own position and wants no rights for others. Louis-Philippe does not receive all the blame and is essentially a good person— but good people do not compensate for the principle of monarchy. Hugo also seeks to fathom the course of the Industrial Revolution, especially the creation of wealth and the distribution of this material production. He likewise seeks a meaning in history and looks for objective clues: "God makes visible to men his will in events, an obscure text written in a mysterious language. . . . Very few minds comprehend the divine tongue." As the reader has previously noted, Hugo does not advance his story in any way by these subjective analyses of his opinions and beliefs, but the novel would not be the fascinating work of art it is without the insertion of his comments on the problems of France during the nineteenth century. At the same time, he charts the initial stages of revolutionary fever in this first book of Part III. He has caught the mood and the infectious enthusiasm of the youths of Paris.

BOOK TWO

After the tumultuous affair in the Thénardier apartment, Marius fled to take shelter with Courfeyrac, one of his young rebel friends. His solemnity, inexplicable to his acquaintances, is the result of the shocking revelation about Thénardier; he still does not know what to do. In fact, he borrows money from Courfeyrac to send to the imprisoned Thénardier every week. The prisoners continue their machinations even inside jail; for them crime is a way of life, and they cannot change their habits even under the eyes of guards. They are primarily concerned about the possibility of escape. Javert, still puzzled about the disappearance of Thénardier's victim, is convinced that the biggest fish escaped the net. Thénardier's two daughters, Eponine and Azelma, are released for lack of sufficient evidence. One day, Marius's old friend Mabeuf receives a visit from Eponine, who is searching for Marius. When Mabeuf directs her to Marius, she tells him the news he sought: Cosette's address. However, Eponine notes sadly that Marius, in love with Cosette, has no regard for her devotion to him.

COMMENT

The scattered interests of the characters are being assembled again by the efforts of some minor characters; in this particular book, Eponine starts to reunite Marius and Cosette. Even Mabeuf, a secondary character, has aided in reestablishing communications between the lovers. Eponine is a Romantic heroine: she is unattractive and far from Marius' ideals, but she has a good heart and suffers from unrequited love. It is interesting to recall the irony of the present circumstance: Eponine and her sister were once beautiful children who cruelly mistreated the neglected and shabby Cosette. Now the tables are turned because of Jean Valjean's goodness toward Cosette, and Eponine is aiding the cause of her forgotten childhood enemy. And yet, Eponine has a spark of humanity; she has blossomed into a kind person in the midst of suffering and misery. Javert lurks, as previously, in the background, and it is evident that he is still on the trail of his victims. The effect is quite different in Part IV: the action is intensified, and the plot unfolds rapidly.

BOOK THREE

Upon Fauchelevent's death, Jean Valjean takes advantage of the situation to leave the convent. He explains to the prioress that he has received a small inheritance from his "brother," and that Cosette is approaching womanhood. To protect himself and Cosette against detection, Jean Valjean rents three houses in Paris that he can use at will. In fact, he spends varying periods of time in the three residences to elude the police. He even becomes a "solid citizen" by serving military duty in the National Guard at periodic intervals. Jean Valjean is happy with Cosette, but he understands that she will leave him some day for a husband. The first premonition of the future occurs in the encounters with Marius in the park of the Luxembourg. Jean Valjean immediately begins to detest this unknown young man who may destroy his present happiness; and he is further upset by Cosette's interest in Marius. The first rift in their idyllic relations is noticeable, and Jean Valjean becomes very depressed. Even the resumption of walks in the park without encountering Marius does not restore the previous felicity between Jean and Cosette. To add to his mental anguish, Jean Valjean sees a group of convicts on their way to the galleys. The horror of the past returns, and the fear of possible capture again terrifies him.

COMMENT

Here, Hugo delicately probes the problem between age and youth, between father and daughter. Jean Valjean's thoughts about the loss of Cosette are uncovered in very sentimental and emotional fashion. Likewise, Cosette's youthful exuberance and the faint stirrings of a first love are viewed from her point of view. Hugo has succeeded in balancing the two points of view: he understands each person's feelings and sympathizes with each individual. Nevertheless, the reader's overall sympathies are with Jean Valjean as the Romantic hero, who is forced to submit to fate and loneliness despite his attempts to surmount all obstacles. Another poignant reminder of the miserable lot of prisoners and the inhumanity of the system of justice—as well as the personal application to the story and Jean Valjean's unhappy life—comes to the fore when he sees the prisoners. Jean's experience and Cosette's innocence are acutely contrasted in the young woman's query, "Father, what are they then, the galley slaves?"

BOOK FOUR

Jean Valjean has secured one triumph from the close call at the Thénardiers: Cosette fondly nurses him back to health from his wounds he suffered in the fight, and their previous strong bonds of affection are restored. After his recovery, Valjean resumes his solitary strolls at twilight to help the poor. One evening, Gavroche, approaching Mabeuf's home, sees Montparnasse, one of the escaped members of the *Patron-Minette* gang, try to mug and rob an old man. The tables are turned: the victim seizes the assailant, lectures him on the punishment that awaits him if he is apprehended by the police, and gives him a purse of money with which to start a new life. The old man is of course Jean Valjean, although the author does not indicate this directly. Montparnasse takes the money, cursing the benefactor and his noble thoughts, but Gavroche picks his pockets and throws the purse into Mabeuf's garden, practically at the startled man's feet. Mabeuf is mystified and can only comment that "this falls from the sky."

COMMENT

Here is a clever note: Gavroche, Mabeuf, and Montparnasse are influenced by each other. The novel's hero, Jean Valjean, is not even mentioned by name; he is treated in secondary fashion in the episode outside Mabeuf's garden. Hugo implies that the laws of coincidence and chance operate on all manner of individuals and in all types of circumstances. People are connected by the mysterious ways of providence, and one may exert control or influence upon others unknowingly. Therefore, everyone should be charitable and operate under the doctrine that his or her acts are important, even the supposedly insignificant ones. Hugo is also preparing his readers for the climactic scenes in which all the characters will have a voice in the action.

BOOK FIVE

Cosette still remembers Marius but is despondent about seeing him again. A handsome cavalry officer, Lieutenant Théodule Gillenormand, passes her house each day, and she is temporarily attracted to him. However, strange incidents are occurring at night: Cosette hears noises in the garden and sees a shadowy figure. Jean Valjean takes no chances and has the gates checked; he is vigilant at night for a time, until he is assured that the police are not on his track. But one evening Cosette notices a stone on the bench she usually sits on; and on the following morning, she guardedly lifts the stone to find a letter.

Despite the lack of any signature, Cosette immediately knows that Marius wrote the love note; however, the letter just consists of phrases extolling the virtues of love. Cosette is transformed into a new person, and she looks at Lieutenant Théodule as an ugly individual. At dusk on that important day, Cosette enters the garden as usual and meets Marius for the first time; they finally exchange names and then declare their love for each other.

COMMENT

The plot takes a major step forward in the meeting of the two lovers. The incidents leading to the garden scene are dramatic and suspenseful. Hugo creates a mysterious mood here. He also cannot resist the temptation to employ the familiar stratagem of coincidence; for example, the lieutenant who flirts with Cosette and could have been a potential rival of Marius is none other than his cousin we met previously. The long, flowery love letter follows the Romantic tradition of the complete dedication of a lover to this sentiment. Love, overpowering in its force and control, must not be treated realistically but poetically. Thus, Hugo writes lyrically in one excerpt of Marius's letter: "Love is the salutation of the angel to the stars," and "O Spring! thou art a letter which I write to her." In the love motif of the novel, Hugo is overwhelmingly on the side of the Romantic viewpoint.

BOOK SIX

In his wanderings about Paris in search of food and shelter, Gavroche ironically helps two youngsters in worse straits than he finds himself in. The two bewildered urchins are Gavroche's brothers who had been "rented out" by their mother for income. From the Gillenormands, the Magnon girl gets a monthly income; and the whole history is another exaggerated coincidence. Gavroche meets Montparnasse, inexpertly disguised, who is planning a prison break for Thénardier and the gang taken by Javert. Thénardier escapes, but the rescue is actually effected by his son, Gavroche, who bravely brings him additional rope to reach the ground.

COMMENT

In his descriptions of the life and environment of the Parisian underworld, Hugo use a great deal of slang, which cannot always be translated. The explanations of the meanings of the words and phrases are paraphrased in notes. This language and descriptions of the dingy and depressing world of the impoverished and depraved inhabitants on the lowest rung of the social ladder create a realistic tone. Thénardier, certainly no fond father, is saved by the daring of his son, who has more human feelings than the parent who gave him life. The irony is Romantic because the opposite effect for Gavroche will be achieved: he is setting loose an evil man who will do him no good and will attempt harm to friends. Although Gavroche will remain a minor figure in the novel, he is emerging as a person with considerable influence over the events of the story. For some unfathomable reason, Gavroche, like his sister, Eponine, has that trace of love in his heart which has not been erased by a hard life. Thus, he also mocks Montparnasse, who is completely unsympathetic, and he protects the two unknown brothers because they are without his resourceful talents.

BOOK SEVEN

This short book is a philosophical and philological pause in the novel. None of the characters, major or minor, appears as the author digresses on the question of slang. There is likewise no action and no development of the plot here.

COMMENT

As a literary exercise, this book is yet another fascinating insight into the wealth of Hugo's thought. The author defends his excursion into the linguistic arena: "*Argot* is the language of misery," and "The historian of morals and ideas has a mission no less austere than that of the historian of events." *Argot,* besides its philological origins, has three explanations: the intrinsic mystery of language which is the direct creation of words; the desire for metaphor or the search for originality of expression; and expedience or the chance and caprice of new words. Hugo is fundamentally a philosopher, and he seeks to explore the relationships between man and language. Thus, he analyzes and concludes that "the idea of man is inseparable from the idea of shade. The night is called *sorgue;* man, *orgue.* Man is a derivative of night." Hugo is likewise mindful of the connection of speech with history so that he muses upon the influence of *argot,* coming from very popular sources, on that great outburst of the people, the French Revolution. And the French Revolution is the hope of humanity: "the ideal armed with the sword . . . closed the door of evil and opened the door of good. . . . It cleared up the question, promulgated truth, drove away miasma, purified the century, crowned the people." From this lyrical and enthusiastic defense of the Revolution of 1789, Hugo leads forward to the next logical bastion of his political philosophy—the necessity of the nineteenth century to continue and advance the work of the French Revolution. What will be the result of these aims and aspirations? The improvement of humanity and the rise of the oppressed classes to the realm of progress and enlightenment. And all this has been developed from an initial reflection upon *argot,* the slang of the Parisian underdogs! As for the style in which he vests his theories and beliefs, Hugo uses hyperbole, metaphor, antithesis—and an optimistic and exuberant state of spirit that is difficult to contradict, as in this celebrated passage:

All progress is tending towards the solution. Some day we shall be astounded. The human race is rising, the lower strata will quite naturally come out from the zone of distress. The abolition of misery will be brought about by a simple elevation of level. This blessed solution, we should do wrong to distrust. The past, it is true, is very strong at the present hour. It is reviving. This revivification of a corpse is surprising. Here it is walking and advancing. It seems victorious; this dead man is a conqueror. He comes with his legion, the superstitions, with his sword, despotism, with his banner, ignorance; within a little time he has won ten battles. He advances, he threatens, he laughs, he is at our doors. As for ourselves, we shall not despair. Let us sell the field whereon Hannibal camped. We who believe, what can we fear? There is no backward flow of ideas more than of rivers. But let those who desire not the future, think of it. In saying no to progress, it is not the future which they condemn, but themselves. They give themselves a melancholy disease; they inoculate themselves with the past. There is but one way of refusing tomorrow, that is to die. Now, no death, that of the body as late as possible, that of the soul never, is what we desire.

BOOK EIGHT

Marius and Cosette meet every evening in the garden of her home, and Jean Valjean suspects nothing about these trysts. Thénardier and the escaped accomplices of the *Patron-Minette* gang are lurking in the vicinity because they have recognized Marius; they seek revenge for their close brush with imprisonment and also sense the opportunity to profit from this enterprise. Eponine, still trying to interest Marius in her own feeble charms to no avail, nevertheless lures her father and his unscrupulous comrades away from the house where Marius enters. When Cosette tells Marius that Jean Valjean has alerted her to a possible sudden departure within a short time, the two decide to run away and get married.

Desperate for money, Marius goes to his grandfather for part of the estate which he should receive some day. A reconciliation almost takes place when Marius calls the old man "father," but the latter's offer to finance his grandson not for marriage to the young woman but to take her as a mistress causes a bitter rebuke from the youth. Marius storms from the house, and old Gillenormand collapses in pitiful frustration at having lost Marius again.

COMMENT

The love affair between Marius and Cosette is rapidly approaching a crisis, and a serious struggle between Jean Valjean and Marius is indicated in Cosette's allegiance to her intended husband rather than to her supposed father. Marius is encountering increasing difficulties because of his precarious financial position and the lack of any promising future. The love story has thus assumed major proportions in this book as the principal plot interest. However, Thénardier and the other ruffians offer a menace which one feels sure has not been eliminated by Eponine's resourcefulness. Eponine and Gillenormand are part of the scaffolding for the love theme. There is considerable reliance upon an emotional reaction from the reader—in the love scenes between Marius and Cosette, the sad plight of Eponine's love for Marius, and Gillenormand's failure at a reunion with his grandson.

BOOK NINE

Jean Valjean has been so preoccupied with his familiar worries that he had not noticed any change in Cosette. On several occasions he has spotted Thénardier and is certain that the rascal is lurking in the neighborhood. Political unrest is mounting in Paris, and Jean Valjean prepares for a flight to England. Also some strange occurrences have annoyed him: the discovery of Marius' address scratched on a wall; and a child's handing to him a note with the single word, "Move." Marius is also distracted because his friends in the political club call for his presence in a street demonstration. Mabeuf honestly returned the purse to the police station, sinks deeper into poverty, and is bewildered by the noise of rioting.

COMMENT

The point of view shifts to the third main character, Jean Valjean; and the collision of all principals comes closer. The net is becoming tighter, and he makes a radical decision to flee France. However, history is now intervening decisively in the affairs of the participants; and the indications of a revolution begin to sweep all the personages along its whirlwind route.

BOOK TEN

Before the action resumes, Hugo cannot resist the urge to explain the peculiar institution of Paris, the *émeute,* or street riot. He traces the history of this phenomenon, the causes for the street insurrections, and the cures for such violent outbursts of public opinion. On June 5, 1832, the funeral of General Lamarque occasioned the *émeute* which is used by Hugo. The demonstrations, generally unorganized and sporadic, became contagious as discontented Parisians swarmed into the streets.

COMMENT

Hugo blames repression as the source of street riots because the more people are forbidden the right to express rationally their views and their possible opposition to a government in power, the more bloody and destructive will be the inevitable showdown with the oppressors. These opinions of Hugo must be viewed in the light of conditions of the nineteenth century in France when very little popular suffrage was granted. Thus he is an accurate prophet of the conditions of his age, and he is even more acute in his analysis of the remedy: "All this is of the past, the future is different. Universal suffrage is so far admirable that it dissolves the *émeute* in its principle, and by giving a vote to insurrection, it takes away its arms. The vanishing of war, of the war of the streets as well as the war of the frontiers, such is inevitable progress. Whatever may be to-day, peace is to-morrow," Nevertheless, Hugo turns a microscopic eye to the outbreak of the Fifth of June and discovers one controlling fact: small incidents may initiate entire revolutionary movements; and when these trifles accumulate, a wave of reaction is established. This is the purpose of the detailed and precise study of the funeral of General Lamarque. At the end of Hugo realizes that no one has grasped what the result would be, and the people have more power in their hands than individual leaders.

BOOK ELEVEN

Gavroche joins in the mischief for the sake of creating more mischief, and he harasses government supporter and rebellious partisan alike. Finally he joins up with the band grouped about Courfeyrac. Even the feeble old man, Mabeuf, has joined the revolutionary forces. Marius is sought but is missing from the rebel ranks.

COMMENT

The tempo of Part IV is picking up speed quickly, and it is apparent that the insurrection of June 5, 1832, is its climax. All the characters, minor to begin with, are being sucked into the vortex of the revolutionary whirlpool. The details of the insurrection are studied for their relation to the mood of the mob and also the specific persons involved.

BOOK TWELVE

The rebels decide to construct a barricade that can be attacked only from the front, on the Rue Saint Denis. Gavroche is eager to join in the coming battle and helps in the building of the barricade. However, in a tall stranger who has entered unnoticed and is likewise working on the fortifications, he recognizes a policeman. Gavroche informs his new friends, and they seize the spy; the prisoner of the rebels admits that he is an officer of the government and that his name is Javert. Enjolras, one of the emerging chiefs of the insurrectionists, announces calmly to Javert that he will be shot ten minutes before the barricade is taken. Enjolras insists that anarchy should not rule; otherwise their struggle is in vain if they cannot bring a better order in place of the present tyrannical regime. Thus he shoots a rebel, really a double agent, who kills a porter.

COMMENT

There is really one contribution in the increasing preparations of the barricade for the plot: the appearance of Javert after a long absence. However, Marius is expected; and his fate is now joined with that of Jean Valjean and Cosette. Eponine, identified only indirectly, is the mysterious intermediary of this book who flits in and out of the fortifications as a messenger. Gavroche has found his milieu, and has also embraced a cause to contain his multiple energies. The revolutionaries in the book are idealists; they are prepared to sacrifice their lives for the future of the revolution. The author gives considerable emphasis to their spirit of cooperation despite any prior political experience, and his sympathies are fully on their side in the uneven engagement with the government forces.

BOOK THIRTEEN

Marius, depressed that he has lost Cosette, winds his way slowly toward the barricade where he decides to die in defense of liberty and in despair about his inability to wed his beloved. Another dilemma plagues the youth: he must die to keep his word of honor to her that life without Cosette was unbearable; and he must not dishonor the memory of his father, hero of so many foreign wars for France, in a civil war that destroys the nation. The state of mind of Marius is "logic mingled with convulsion."

COMMENT

The mental conflict for Marius—a variation of the anguish that afflicted him in Part III at the Thénardier affair—becomes a source for Hugo's commentary upon civil war. Civil war is only an extension of foreign war, and all warfare is against the highest interests of humanity. Hugo is a pacifist who believes that as mankind strives onward and upward, reason and civilization will banish war from the earth. The wars of Napoleon were feats of great achievement, but the French Revolution, in an attack upon a corrupt system, was far superior: "To conquer at Austerlitz is grand; to take the Bastille is immense."

BOOK FOURTEEN

The attack on the barricade commences with a furious assault by government troops. Mabeuf, the eighty-year-old veteran of the French Revolution, volunteers to restore the fallen flag; but he is killed by enemy soldiers. Marius enters the fortifications in time to save Gavroche and Courfeyrac from being shot by snipers. However, the superiority of the trained troops gradually overcomes the insurrectionists; only the courage of Marius in threatening to blow up the barricade with ignited powder forces the soldiers to retreat. Marius is acknowledged as the leader of the rebels, and he now accepts his fate as a member of the insurrection. Eponine calls feebly to him; she has placed her hand over the musket of a soldier as he was about to fire at Marius and the girl is dying. She recognizes Gavroche, her brother, and does the last service to her unrequited lover by delivering a letter to him from Cosette.

Cosette informs Marius of the temporary new address Jean Valjean and she will have before they flee to England in a week. In order to save Gavroche from death or capture, Marius sends the urchin to Cosette with a reply in which he states his intention to perish for their impossible love. However, Gavroche leaves with the intention of returning quickly to the barricade.

COMMENT

Marius is now firmly committed to the battle and is thus a foe of Javert although the latter is held a prisoner by the rebels. The mysterious and contagious enthusiasm of men at war is sketched favorably; the little incidents of a conflict, such as the sacrifice of Mabeuf for the flag and Marius' assumption of leadership, are realistically drawn. Hugo has tried to understand not only the actions in themselves but also the psychology and the motivations of individuals prepared to fight and die. He clearly appeal to the audience for sympathy, and the reader cannot but hope for the escape—somehow—of these brave, doomed idealists. If the above depictions are in a realistic vein, the death of Eponine is pure Romanticism; for example, she tenderly says to Marius: "Promise to kiss me on the forehead when I am dead. I shall feel it. . . . And then, do you know, Monsieur Marius, I believe I was a little in love with you." In addition to this skillful balancing of Romantic traits and a broad realism, Hugo has adhered to another dictum of Romanticism: the mixing of tragic and comic elements together. Thus, Gavroche—the wayward brother of the pitiful Eponine—

comes into the scene after her death; likes the activity of war; admires his new-found friends; and will not take the orders of Marius without expressing his own puckish will.

BOOK FIFTEEN

Jean Valjean, in his departure for one of his other residences, has had the first real quarrel of his life with Cosette. But he is terrified to remain even in Paris and remembers the note with the word "Move." He does not know that Eponine sent that message in her confessed attempt to separate Marius and Cosette. Valjean and Cosette, although they do not argue openly now, maintain a cold silence. That evening he finds the explanation for Cosette's conduct: the news of the trip to another house and eventually to England is reflected in the mirror from the blotter on the desk. Valjean is stunned, and sinks into a period of melancholy and reverie. At last, he puts on his uniform of the National Guard and leaves the house; he meets Gavroche, suspects another communication when the youngster asks him for the address, and claims the message is for him. Despite some anxiety, Gavroche hands over the letter in order to hasten back to the barricade. Jean is still more crushed when he reads the tender words of Marius' farewell to Cosette. He departs once more. Gavroche, still the mischievous little insurrectionist, steals a cart for the barricade but is forced to use it as a battering ram against interfering troops.

COMMENT

In this last book of the very lengthy Part IV, Jean Valjean appears as the major character he is; and the novelist probes the inner workings and the tragic fate of his hero. Once more, the whole, delicate world of Jean Valjean is collapsing: Cosette is in love with Marius and will leave him, and he must make a grave decision between humanitarianism and self-interest. For the first time in his many trials, Jean admits defeat—"Jean Valjean till this day had never been vanquished when put to the proof." Hatred versus love struggle in his soul, and the admonitions of Bishop Myriel are put to their severest test after so many years when Valjean thought he would never again relapse into evil. If he conceals the letter and flees with Cosette, she will think her lover unfaithful or dead; and he will then have his daughter, for he cannot conceive her as otherwise than his own child, with him in safety.

Yet can he live with his conscience and in the light of the good prelate's words? How does a man come to a fateful and major choice in life? Hugo, in one of his most striking passages of psychological analysis, hints at the mysterious hand of providence and charity: "There are some mechanical impulses which come to us, without our knowledge even, from our deepest thoughts. It was doubtless under the influence of an impulse of this kind, and of which he was hardly conscious, that Jean Valjean five minutes afterwards found himself in the street." And to offset this serious and tragic interlude, Hugo inserts the humorous adventure of Gavroche with the cart as he attacks a group of government troops—an episode which Hugo ironically observes has gone down in the annals of the insurrection as the "nocturnal attack on the post of the Imprimerie Royale." The vignette is a practical example of Hugo's previously noted concept of history and rebellions: small, unrelated, and unplanned events are never understood fully by the participants; and revolutions are inflamed by a series of these minute happenings.

GENERAL COMMENTARY

Part IV, the longest of the five parts of *Les Misérables,* has as its title "St. Denis," which is explained toward the conclusion of the whole section. The insurrection is centered on this particular street of Paris; and the rebellion is rapidly bringing all the characters, major and minor, together. Thus, Marius and Javert are already inside the barricade: the former is the leader of the group of rebels; and the latter, a prisoner of the insurrectionists, has by necessity become the foe of the young man as a representative of crime. It is quite obvious also that Jean Valjean is on his way to the barricade. Only Cosette remains out of sight and unaware of what is transpiring. The story and the plot have assumed a dynamic quality as Hugo shifts back and forth during a short period of time.

Time is very compressed now: everything occurs within the space of a few hours. Hugo has selected a background of high drama for his characters: a typical street demonstration arising at the familiar cry of "To the barricades!" Until this time, there has been very little dramatic involvement of the personages; perhaps after the exciting climax at the Thénardiers, a period of relative calm was required. In fact, the minor characters, such as Gavroche and Eponine, carry on much of the story's progress. It is therefore probably no accident that Hugo sketched them as brother and sister: for the antithesis and for the combining power of chance at play.

The love theme predominates in the first half of the part, and the main focus is on the developing passion between Marius and Cosette. In the second half of Part IV, Jean Valjean and Javert, still in the background, begin to enter the fray. Although there are the usual digressions of Hugo in this part, there is also great technical mastery of the art of the novel in this swing of the pendulum between major and minor characters and the two principal plots of the novel: the love of Marius and Cosette, and the chase of Jean Valjean by Javert.

Nevertheless, all the many digressive elements of the first four parts of *Les Misérables* begin to make sense now: Hugo is building a political theory and a philosophy of history from these extensive and detailed detours. Thus there are three diversionary ideas in the fourth part in the construction of the novelist's thought: the historical background of the Bourbons and their fall from power in 1830; the critique of *argot* as connotative of the popular spirit; and the contribution of the *émeute* as symptomatic of the ills of the past and the hope of the future. Hugo is an optimist and a firm believer in progress; and these ideas, already observed and commented upon previously, are brought more emphatically and logically to the reader's comprehension in Part Four. Although he is a pacifist, Hugo believes that the present oppressive political situation can be remedied only by insurrections. When the people have the franchise, then reason and good sense will provide the backdrop for an enlightened government—and any changes in administration later—to effect the climb toward a golden age of humanity.

Whether or not one agrees with Hugo in his approach to history and the future, one can hardly deny that he is stimulating and prophetic in his writing. Without bold pens such as Hugo's, the fight for reform and democracy in France and Europe during the nineteenth century would not have made the achievements it did. And his ideas still deserve consideration today.

PART V: JEAN VALJEAN

BOOK ONE

At two o'clock on the following morning, only thirty-seven rebels are left to man the barricade; food and water are also running short, and the end of resistance is only a matter of time. Still idealistic, the leaders want those who are married and the sole support of families to escape in uniforms of the National Guard which the insurrectionists have captured. Five are ordered from the ranks, but only four uniforms are available until a stranger casts in a fifth outfit. Marius is astonished to see Jean Valjean disrobe to save another man. Jean Valjean had entered the street easily because of his identification as a loyalist. Enjolras harangues the dispirited revolutionaries with the noble sacrifice they are making for future citizens. Marius and Jean Valjean exchange no words after Marius had identified Valjean laconically: "I know him." Inside, Jean Valjean and Javert face each other; the tables have been turned, for now the former is the captor and the policeman the prisoner.

Javert is no coward and haughtily acknowledges his elusive prey's presence thus: "It is very natural." Meanwhile, the government forces have brought up a small cannon with which they intend to demolish the barricade and then storm the remnants of the stronghold with infantry. The rebels fire at the artillerymen to prevent shots from being hurled, but the fortification is gradually reduced to ruins. Gavroche enters and does not recognize Jean Valjean in the daylight. The *gamin* of Paris does his last good act and trick: he jumps outside to gather cartridges for the rebels and taunts the soldiers with mocking songs, but the enemy bullets have the last say and kill him. Last preparations are made for the rebels to fight the troops and attempt escape. As a reward for his services, Jean Valjean asks for Javert—"To blow out that man's brains myself." But Javert is just as arrogant and courageous in his reaction—"That is appropriate." Jean Valjean leads Javert away, unties him, and explains: "You are free." In addition, he gives the policeman his address. His action breaks Javert psychologically. "You annoy me," he says. "Kill me rather." Jean Valjean replies simply, "Go away." After firing a shot in the air to deceive the rebels, Valjean rejoins the group. Marius, having learned from Enjolras the name of the policeman, is in a quandary when he sees Jean Valjean come back. Now comes the final assault upon the barricade, and Enjolras bravely faces an execution squad for his role in the rebellion. All the others are dead, wounded, or prisoners. Marius has been under the watchful eye of Jean Valjean; when the young man is shot, Valjean grabs him up and flees. All escape routes are blocked, so Valjean opens the grating in the street that leads to the Paris sewers.

COMMENT

This first book of the last part of the novel is melodramatic and climactic. The background of the fierce combat between insurrectionists and loyalists is sketched vividly, yet Hugo takes the time to comment upon the great *émeute* (uprising) that he witnessed—that of 1848, which completely toppled the monarchy in France. In fact, the doomed insurrection of 1832 taught the later rebels some valuable lessons for their successful revolt. Hugo is very proud of what 1848 accomplished, and he ranks that date with 1789, when the French Revolution broke out, as a glorious year in the emancipation of humanity. Thus, the fight at St. Denis probably represents factual information that Hugo had gathered from contemporary accounts and from the experience of the success of 1848. He is perhaps hinting at how his foe, Napoleon III, might be toppled from power as were the Bourbons. Hugo is still the Romantic: the deaths of Gavroche, Enjolras, and the other patriots are stirring and melodramatic. Also, at the moment of Gavroche's demise, Hugo shifts the scene to see what the two urchin brothers are doing; these two youngsters have to steal bread that a bourgeois tossed to the birds in the pond. The older one now takes charge of the younger, as Gavroche had done. Cosette is fleetingly depicted, uneasy but unaware of the fate of Jean Valjean and Marius.

The story has returned to the first plot: the pursuit and flight theme, the confrontation between Jean Valjean and Javert. The former has triumphed over himself, as the last book of the preceding part hinted, and Combeferre, one of the young rebels, indicated this fact upon noticing Jean's handing over of his uniform: "He is a man who saves others." During the battle of the barricade, Jean Valjean avoids killing the enemy by shooting close to them so that they withdraw— another curiosity noted by the rebels. The very theatrical but psychologically motivated encounter between Jean Valjean and Javert ends in victory for Valjean. Javert, from the beginning of his chase of Jean Valjean, has been puzzled by this criminal who does not behave as a criminal. In the narrow view of the police inspector, all criminals fit one pattern; he cannot comprehend that this man is no criminal. Thus, his whole set of values crumbles, and he begs to die: death would be a vindication of his creed. Beyond a doubt, this meeting of the two personages is a highlight of the entire novel. The rendition of Jean Valjean as a Romantic here is fully justified. However, he must do one additional act of goodness: the rescue of Marius so that the young man can be reunited with Cosette.

If in terms of action this episode is not the climax of the novel, it is certainly so in terms of mental conflict and the clash of ideas. Hugo pays an enthusiastic eulogy to the fallen barricade by asserting that it has served the progress and the honor of France.

BOOK TWO

No action occurs, and none of the characters appears in this book, which is devoted completely to the history of the sewers of Paris.

COMMENT

This digressive commentary on the sewers of Paris is one of the famous excerpts from *Les Misérables,* because it contains so many of Hugo's technical devices and is a compelling example of his poetical talent. Here, he takes an uncommon and ugly aspect of the city and transforms it into a fascinating object of study through his purple prose, metaphors, hyperbole, and lyrical phraseology. The book of the sewers is both Romantic and Realistic: the history and present statistics, together with the rather unpleasant aspect in general of this underground mechanism, convince the reader that Hugo has done considerable research and speaks authoritatively. At the same time, the style and the philosophical ideas extracted from the sewers are in the tradition of the Romantics. For example, this notable paragraph is often cited as typical of Hugo's brilliance in poetic prose:

We might say that, for ten centuries, the cloaca has been the disease of Paris. The sewer is the taint which the city has in her blood. The popular instinct is never mistaken. The trade of sewerman was formerly almost as perilous, and almost as repulsive to the people, as the trade of knacker so long stricken with horror, and abandoned to the executioner. It required high wages to persuade a mason to disappear in that fetid ooze; the welldigger's ladder hesitated to plunge into it; it was said proverbially: to descend into the sewer is to

enter the grave; and all manner of hideous legends, as
we have said, covered this colossal drain with dismay;
awful sink, which bears the traces of the revolutions
of the globe as well as of the revolutions of men, and
in which we find vestiges of all the cataclysms from
the shellfish of the deluge down to the rag of Marat.

BOOK THREE

The journey Jean Valjean makes carrying the wounded and
unconscious Marius through the filthy sewers is perilous
from natural and unnatural sources. The authorities have
surmised that some rebels might try to escape through the
sewers, and Valjean notices behind him eight or ten black
uniforms. He eludes them successfully but he is bewildered
by the maze of this subterranean passage. Marius is heavy
to carry; Valjean is tired; the stench and slime of the sewers
nauseate the brave man. At last, he makes a turn in the right
direction and sees a grating leading to the outside. But he
cannot open it from the inside. All seems lost at the point of
freedom when Thénardier offers release for Jean and Marius.
Jean Valjean recognizes Thénardier but the latter does not
know his opponent because of Valjean's silent manner and
disheveled condition. Thénardier takes them out because he
sees the occasion for a little blackmail: in his warped, criminal mind, one must be murderer and the other victim.

Unfortunately Valjean has only thirty francs with him, and
Thénardier stealthily rips off a piece of cloth from Marius'
coat for future use. For Thénardier, this affair has been
profitable in one way, because he has avoided the police
who are on his trail; he has given them another quarry. In
fact, after Thénardier's departure, Jean Valjean only momen-
tarily enjoys freedom: he is soon facing the gaze of the police—in the person of Javert. The police inspector does not
associate this grimy individual with his prey of long standing
until Jean identifies himself. Then, of course, Javert in a rage
seizes Valjean, and the three protagonists come together—

"the three tragic immobilities, the corpse, the spectre, and the statue." Javert believes that Marius is dead and allows Jean Valjean to take him home—the address being conveniently located in the youth's coat.

After this errand of mercy, Jean has one further last request: to go to his own home for a short time. The morose and solemn Javert strangely accedes to this wish and even waits outside; however, Valjean, looking out the window a few moments later, is bewildered by Javert's disappearance. Meanwhile, Marius is received with joy by the Gillenormands; although the young man has been very seriously wounded and needs urgent medical attention, he is alive.

COMMENT

The long-awaited confrontation of the three characters has taken place, and it is now quite easy to determine who is the hero or the central protagonist of *Les Misérables*. Marius is unconscious and is considered dead by Javert; indeed, the young rebel has been only a passive presence in this book so far. Javert is in the throes of agonizing capitulation because he has had to face the issue that Jean Valjean is no criminal according to his definition. This man is different, and Javert says little. His concession of the two favors requested is completely out of character for the ruthless pursuer of wrongdoers. In fact, Javert is indirectly breaking the law and could be affording a culprit the opportunity to escape.

Javert's abandonment of his post outside Jean Valjean's house is clearly a retreat from the battlefield. Jean Valjean, suffering terribly at the vision of this return to the galleys, does not realize his victory over Javert; he does recognize his triumph over himself and for that reason can never contemplate suicide: "Suicide, that mysterious assault upon the unknown, which may contain, in a certain measure, the death of the soul, was impossible to Jean Valjean." This thought is key when Hugo follows Javert to his doom in the next book. Here is the comparison and contrast of two persons and two philosophies, and here is victory and defeat. There will be no more great crises for Jean Valjean in his adherence to Bishop Myriel's idealism; he has emerged as the Romantic hero—but with a profound and realistic psychological penetration.

Thénardier, that menace, comes into the action once more—by coincidence—with the implication that he will utilize that piece of torn cloth from Marius. One happy event occurs: the reunion of the Gillenormands with Marius, although it has taken a close brush with death to effect the reconciliation.

BOOK FOUR

Javert dominates this short book, which exposes the nakedness of his rigid ideas. He cannot admit of change in his credo, and he certainly cannot grant that: "A convict was his benefactor. . . . Terrible situation! To be moved." At last, he writes a letter to the police administration about reforms in the handling of convicts and the accused—which are only technical points and never delve into the problem of the criminal mind and the possibility of innocence. He places his hat carefully on the edge of the quai, or bank, of the river Seine and jumps to his death.

COMMENT

It is probably a failure in the novel that the character and personality of Javert have been neglected until this brief scene of his last moments. But within these few pages, Hugo masterfully analyzes all the conflicting doubts of the police inspector; he brings all the unusual characteristics of Jean Valjean to bear upon the Javert's thinking. Javert is a symbol of the law without any regard for the individual and without the employment of humanitarian and charitable virtues. Besides a striking study of an individual, the portrait of Javert in the throes of collapse is a stunning condemnation of a society that bases its strength upon the externals of law and justice without the internal qualities of love and mercy. The Infinite and the Unknown have no place in Javert's creed and in the social order; the police inspector remarks to himself: "But how manage to send in his resignation to God?" With the death of Javert, Jean Valjean is free, but at the end of Book Four he still does not know this. Nevertheless, the theme of pursuit and flight ends here; the chase is over as far as the haunting menace of Javert is concerned.

BOOK FIVE

Jean Valjean digs up the treasure he has kept concealed for many years and is observed only by an old peasant—who recalls a similar situation many years ago. Marius and the Gillenormands are firmly reconciled; Jean comes to inquire about him every day; and the grandfather gives permission for the young man to marry Cosette. Jean Valjean gives Cosette a dowry of almost 600,000 francs, and the Gillenormands accept her even more willingly. Jean Valjean has also read in the newspapers about the death of Javert. However, he feels compelled to tell Cosette he is not her father; so her illegitimacy will not be known, he tells her she is the daughter of Fauchelevent. She accepts this sad news about Jean Valjean and the lie about her supposed father because she is so in love with Marius that nothing else matters.

Marius is increasingly preoccupied about the mysterious Jean Valjean; all his probing inquiries fail to elicit any information from Cosette's guardian. At the same time, Marius wants to find out the name of the man who saved his life during the battle at the barricade.

COMMENT

In this book, the story takes a more optimistic direction. Javert's death has finally freed Jean Valjean from the police officer's implacable hatred and relentless pursuit. There is consequently a noticeable slackening of suspense and excitement. All the strands of the plot are coming rapidly together: the Gillenormands and Marius, Marius and Cosette, and Jean Valjean's last encounter with fate in the person of Cosette's fiancé. Despite the apparent happiness of the group, the cloud of doubt hovering about Marius is a clear foreshadowing of more trouble for Jean Valjean. This future woe is indicated by the docile and tired attitude of the old man; it is also increased by the place in Cosette's heart which Marius assumes. Thus it is evident that Jean's bliss is only superficial.

BOOK SIX

On Feb. 16, 1833, Marius and Cosette are married—eight months after Jean Valjean carried the wounded youth to his grandfather's home from the barricade and the sewer. The wedding festivities are held in the traditional aristocratic and upper-middle-class fashion that befits the Gillenormands. Cosette is radiantly happy and does not notice Jean Valjean's melancholy look. He has given as a dowry to Marius almost all the wealth he had accumulated by hard work during the years at M____ sur M____. During the wedding banquet, he disappears—and is only slightly missed.

Valjean returns to his old place of residence and sobs fearfully; all the old temptations between goodness and evil again plague him. He looks at the ragged clothes that Cosette was wearing when he rescued her years ago. He also realizes that he has no place in the social sphere that Cosette now inhabits; his very presence in her society is a disturbing factor to the aspirations of Marius and the Gillenormands. In short, Jean Valjean "had reached the last crossing of good and evil. He had that dark intersection before his eyes. This time again, as it had already happened him to in other sorrowful crises, two roads opened before him; the one tempting, the other terrible. Which should he take?"

COMMENT

Jean Valjean returns to the center of the novel's stage, and the situation is a typical example of Romantic irony. He has worked for many years for the happiness of Cosette, and the day of her wedding should have been the culmination of these many dreams. Nevertheless, Jean knows that he is not wanted by Marius and the Gillenormands and that he is an outsider in the glittering world of the bourgeois circles of the Restoration. The descriptions of these solid citizens and their activities are likewise ironic portrayals by Hugo of the society of 1833. Jean Valjean is still a "miserable one," and an outcast such as he cannot be accepted by the middle class. Cosette has passed from one social class to another, and Valjean knows that her background will always be suspect as long as he remains. Hugo emphatically traces Valjean's psychological agony in a series of pitiless questions, repetitive but forceful, which evoke the reader's sympathy and understanding. Although the analysis of Jean's feelings is artistically drawn, the appeal is frankly and constantly sentimental in the best tradition of the Romantics. Thus, Hugo can describe the mental torments of Jean Valjean by means of this realistic and detailed metaphorical device: "Martyrdom is a sublimation, a corrosive sublimation. It is a torture of consecration. You consent to it the first hour; you sit upon the throne of red-hot iron, you put upon your brow the crown of red-hot iron, you receive the globe of red-hot iron, you take the sceptre of red-hot iron, but you have yet to put on the mantle of flame, and is there no moment when the wretched flesh revolts, and when you abdicate the torture?"

BOOK SEVEN

The day after the wedding, Jean Valjean returns to the Gillenormand residence and confesses to Marius that he is a wanted former convict. Marius, incredulous at first, is unable to understand why Jean Valjean does not remain silent about his past. The old man answers calmly that his only motive is that of honor, and he will vanish from Cosette's life because he can do nothing more for her. He even rejects Marius's offer to secure a pardon through family contacts because the authorities already believe him dead. He argues with stirring voice that "To live, once I stole a loaf of bread; to-day, to live, I will not steal a name."

As Marius recalls his previous doubts and fears about Jean Valjean, and as the memory of Thénardier comes to mind, he shows mounting antipathy to Cosette's guardian. The appearance of Cosette only briefly indicates some possibility of a reconciliation between Jean Valjean and Marius. When she departs, Marius eagerly accepts Valjean's offer not to see her again. Infuriated at such ingratitude, Valjean begs to see her from time to time; and Marius consents to his appearance at the house each evening for a short visit.

When Jean Valjean takes his leave, Marius is "completely unhinged" at the astounding news he has just heard and also at the obvious sincerity and honestly of Jean Valjean. In fact, Marius regrets the concession of the daily visit to Cosette; and he concludes cruelly that "after the lowest of men, comes the convict. . . . He should have merely and simply cast off Jean Valjean."

COMMENT

In a pitiful and emotional speech to Marius, Jean Valjean sums up all his suffering: "I am of no family. I am not of yours. I am not of the family of men. In houses where people are at home I am an incumbrance. There are families, but they are not for me. I am the unfortunate; I am outside. . . . To be happy, I! Have I the right to be happy? I am outside of life, monsieur." It is clear that the old man is succumbing to the final blow of his life: the loss of Cosette and the rejection by Marius, the man whose life he has saved. Jean is still true to the ideals of Bishop Myriel, but the cost to his spirit as he grows older and troubles mount is enormous. He is a man who sacrifices all for love and charity; on the outside, he is repulsive and a criminal, but on the inside, he is the epitome of idealism.

Marius offers the other side of the coin: this young man, handsome, wealthy, and with all the social advantages, lacks any understanding of human nature. He has the veneer of social polish but is wanting in inner virtues; he is a prototype of the bourgeois values of the Restoration which Hugo so bitterly condemns. The scene between Jean Valjean and Marius is a sharp contrast in the problem of appearance and reality; and the attraction is very sentimental and tragic. However, the points of view shift to that one follows the trajectory of Marius's thought and attitudes. By now, the reader is well aware of the dilemma in the young man's mind: how can he reconcile devotion to his father by loyalty to the scoundrel, Thénardier, with a debt to Jean Valjean as Cosette's guardian? The sole problem for the audience is a possible solution for this impasse.

BOOK EIGHT

Jean Valjean's visits to Cosette are conducted on a very formal level; for example, he insists that she call him not "father" but "Monsieur Jean." He in turn calls her "madame" and not "Cosette." This behavior surprises and hurts Cosette a great deal. From Cosette's remarks, he gradually realizes that Marius is trying to live on his own income and not use any of the dowry. Although Cosette misses him during an absence of two days in the visitations, she is so occupied with her new role as wife and housekeeper that she swiftly adjusts to the brief separation. Jean resumes the interviews, but his spirit is evidently weakened by the mental strain he is undergoing. His whole way of life is slowing down, due to the breakdown of his health.

COMMENT

The partial solution to the novelist's problem is now rather apparent in the references to Jean Valjean's declining physical strength. The frosty greetings and icy dialogue between Jean and Cosette provide a logical explanation for the old man's loss of the will to live. Charged with high emotion, the scenes avoid some charge of melodrama because Valjean's reactions are a consequence of his adherence to Bishop Myriel's ideals of sacrifice and love.

BOOK NINE

Marius gradually withdraws Cosette from her attention and interest in Jean Valjean; the young woman is so much in love with her husband that she freely consents to his wishes. Valjean at last falls ill and remains in bed; he is unable to eat, and a doctor confirms the seriousness of his illness. Valjean struggles to write a letter to Cosette, in which he explains that her dowry was honestly gained through the profits of his factory under the name of Madeleine. Meanwhile, Thénardier, disguised as a respectable citizen, seeks a meeting with Marius. The latter, penetrating the rascal's disguise without any difficulty, confronts him with his true name and unsavory reputation. Eager to blackmail Marius in order to get money for a swift departure from France. Thénardier claims he knows the truth about Jean Valjean.

To Thénardier's claims about Valjean's true identity and past prison record, Marius assents that he already knows these facts. In fact, Marius counterclaims by saying that Jean killed a certain Madeleine to acquire money and later murdered a police inspector, Javert, who was on his trail. Thénardier, who originally came to attack Jean Valjean, feels proud to correct Marius; he proves by newspapers that Jean was Madeleine and that Javert committed suicide. Marius is stunned by these documents of Jean's innocence, but Thénardier tries to destroy his growing happiness. Thénardier relates that Jean Valjean, despite his innocence of the crimes suspected by Marius, is really a murderer and thief. Of course, Thénardier gives in detail all the events of Marius's rescue from the barricade by Jean; the proof of Thénardier on this occasion is the missing piece of cloth from Marius' coat. Marius, overjoyed at this vindication of Jean, explains proudly to Thénardier that "You came to accuse this man, you have justified him; you wanted to destroy him, you have succeeded only in glorifying him."

Marius rids himself and his conscience of Thénardier by giving him some money to rehabilitate himself—Thénardier uses the funds to become a slave-trader. For Marius, "the convict was transfigured into Christ," and he rushes to Cosette with the joyful news of his faith in Jean Valjean. Marius and Cosette hasten to see the ill Valjean, and Marius begs pardon of the old man for his harsh treatment. Jean explains that the dowry was not stolen money, and he also tells Cosette about her unknown mother, Fantine. He refuses a priest on his deathbed and simply points upward to indicate that he believes in God and in Bishop Myriel. He is stoical at the end and states that "it is nothing to die; it is frightful not to live." His wish to have no stone over his grave is obeyed, and Jean Valjean was buried in the neighborhood of the potters' field.

COMMENT

Thénardier, cause of much of the misery and tragic circumstances of Jean Valjean, becomes in this last book the source of his short, final happiness. The case is highly ironic as Marius corrects Thénardier in his accusations, and Thénardier then shows Marius the error of his assumptions. In fact, Thénardier, who has showed himself a complete scoundrel, says very seriously: "Before all things, truth and justice. I do not like to see people accused unjustly." The evidence of the piece of cloth is of course another employment of coincidence to support the plot.

The transformation of Marius is in accord with the concept of the sweeping goodness of Jean Valjean and the ideals first set in motion by Bishop Myriel. The deathbed scene, uniting the three protagonists, has been prepared by various references to Jean Valjean's declining health, but the episode is totally sentimental and melodramatic. The confession of Marius, Jean's steadfast loyalty to humanitarianism and sacrifice, Cosette's tears—all are strictly in the Romantic credo. Nevertheless, Hugo has the courage to include his own religious beliefs; he makes the point clearly and emphatically that the love of God is individualistic and outside of formal religion. Jean Valjean's last words to Marius and Cosette are the affirmation and espousal of his life's work. And the unmarked, obscure grave denotes him as a "misérable," or outcast, that is to say, a Romantic hero.

GENERAL COMMENTARY

This last part is the most dynamic and dramatic of the entire novel as the barricade is breached, Jean Valjean rescues Marius, and the flight through the sewers of Paris takes place. This last element, perhaps one of the most famous descriptive passages of *Les Misérables,* is one of the highlights of Hugo's literary output. The end of the chase comes in the overwhelming psychological defeat of Javert and in his suicide. There are several melodramatic and exaggerated aspects to the climax, but the sentiments are so strongly expressed that the technical defects are forgiven. And yet,

Hugo has delicately balanced his actions with advance indications of changes in his characters. Before the fifth part, Javert had already begun to waver in his rigid adherence to the code of law, order and discipline untempered by any human warmth. It was likewise inevitable that all the characters should be brought together against the backdrop of a great political and social upheaval.

When Javert disappears from the story, Cosette takes his place to complete the triangle. From the police inspector's suicide, a new phase of Part V develops. In this second structural division, the interest is centered on the love story between Marius and Cosette—although the latter's personality is always somewhat effaced. The central conflict now is between Marius and Jean Valjean, and of course the latter triumphs totally. For that reason, Hugo probably entitled the fifth part with the name of his hero. Hugo is a careful novelist in that he has solved all the mysteries of his plot and has left no part without an ending. However, he has had to strain here as throughout *Les Misérables*. Certainly he violates many canons of the laws of probability and possibility, but he does so to build an overwhelming effect of sympathy for Jean Valjean and the noble ideals he has inherited from Bishop Myriel.

In Part V, Hugo has eliminated most of the philosophical digressions that were so noticeable in the other parts of the novel. Only in the brilliant and fascinating spectacle of the sewers of Paris does he digress to give one of the best examples of his writing. Like a good dramatist—and it may be recalled that Hugo gained laurels in the theater before seriously attempting the novel—he must conclude his story very rapidly once it reaches its climax. Thus, the marriage of Cosette and Marius, Jean Valjean's vindication, and his death occur very quickly. But the novelist cannot resist a final thrust at some of his old foes, and in the death of Jean Valjean he sees this occasion. Jean Valjean's affirmation of a belief in God as an outside force parallels Hugo's own concept in the explanation of the battle of Waterloo. Likewise, there is no need for organized religion, although the religious ideals of Bishop Myriel are the basis and foundation of Jean Valjean's life.

Finally, Hugo defends the anonymity of the grave and the falseness of society in placing such faith in external manifestations such as large and expensive cemeteries and tombstones. Hugo's ideas met much opposition from orthodox and conservative critics during his own lifetime; his ideas, as summarized in Valjean's deathbed scene, are certainly provocative and worthy of careful attention. Even at the risk of opposition, Hugo had the courage to state his ideas and ideals. Whether the reader adheres to the same principles or disagrees with Victor Hugo can be proved only by a careful and appreciative reading of the whole text—for which a summary and a commentary are only a guide and not a substitute.

CRITICAL COMMENTARY

Victor Hugo believed firmly in the outstanding merit of *Les Misérables* as his masterpiece, but he was also aware of the difficulties which the novel would create. Thus he at first refused to release the book in serial form for fear that the total effect of the work of art might be lost; and he rejected all editorial suggestions that he shorten the philosophical passages. He accurately forecast the impact of *Les Misérables* when he wrote to his publisher: "The quick-moving surface drama will be a success for twelve months; the deeper drama, for twelve years."

The novel proved an immediate and immense success, and Hugo gained large royalties, more than he ever had received previously—and more than his literary contemporaries had been acquiring. Public reaction showed that *Les Misérables* touched the issues of the age, and a friend, Paul Meurice, wrote to Hugo: "For the last six days all Paris has been reading, devouring, *Les Misérables*. It is obvious from the first talk about the book, and such small comments as have as yet appeared in the press, that the first effect, as was easy to forecast, has been immense. Everyone is raving! Everyone is carried away! There is a complete absence of petty objections and pedantic reservations. The crushing weight of so much grandeur, justice, and sovereign compassion is all that counts. It is quite irresistible."

ADVERSE REACTION

Not all commentators found the novel so irresistible, however. Some of the unflattering reactions ranged from a personal attack on Hugo as the "leading demagogue of France" to Baudelaire's bitter comment that "this unspeakably foul and stupid book . . . Hugos's whole family, and his disciples, fill me with horror." Even Lamartine, once a literary and political idol of Hugo, penned this damaging review: "This is a dangerous book. . . . The masses can be infected by no more murderous, no more terrible, passion than a passion for the impossible." Gradually, critics adopted a more balanced view; and Théophile Gautier concluded judiciously about the novel that "It is neither good nor bad; it is no handiwork of man but a phenomenon of natural forces." Critical reaction can still be harsh toward Hugo's book, and Albert George states: "Hugo continued the worst elements of the romance recipe because he gave so little thought to his prose, an effect that would also show up in *Les Misérables.*" Nevertheless, Andre Maurois adds this personal note on the novel's influence: "When I was fifteen, I was completely bowled over by *Les Misérables.* All my life long I have continually been discovering fresh aspects of his genius." Maurois in his biography of Hugo writes later of *Les Misérables*: "Time has now delivered its verdict. *Les Misérables* has come to be accepted by the whole world as one of the great works of the human imagination."

ASPECTS OF THE NOVEL

The human imagination that Hugo demonstrated at such great length in *Les Misérables* may be seen in the way that the novel has been assigned to several forms of the genre; indeed, one of the chief qualities of *Les Misérables* resides in the fact that it is a synthesis of existing aspects of the novel. Thus, *Les Misérables* is a detective story, a story of war and revolution, a love story, a romantic novel, a realistic novel, a religious novel, and a philosophical novel. Hugo has succeeded in writing an epic in prose—something that he attempted in poetry and never fully brought off. Despite the various types of novel in *Les Misérables,* there is outstanding artistic unity; and Hugo defined his ambitions about this book thus: "This book has been composed from within to outward: the idea giving birth to the characters, the characters producing the drama—there is the law of art."

A DETECTIVE STORY

School adaptations and movie versions have stressed the struggle between Jean Valjean and Javert; the pursuit and flight of the police inspector and the suspect are in the best spirit of the detective story genre which developed rapidly in the nineteenth century. It is very true that this conflict is central to all the action and contains all the traits of suspense and thrills. However, it is not the principal issue as far as the author is concerned; and the main ideas are not those of the usual detective story. Nevertheless, Javert is a model detective; his relentless chase of his victim is in the tradition of all the great sleuths of the past and of the present—from Sherlock Holmes down to the present.

Javert is, however, more than an ordinary policeman; he is a disturbed individual who brings to his unpleasant work a distorted sense of duty. Although Javert is unfortunately not developed in all the myriad turns and twists of his warped personality, he is nevertheless a memorable figure. In other words, the usual detective story, built around the plot, is not presented here because Javert stands forth as a fascinating character. But the detective story is pursued with melodrama, suspense, and thrills from Javert's first encounter with Madeleine to the his suicide. The high point is, of course, the chase through the sewers of Paris; all the elements of excitement and danger are involved in this chapter. Another peak of reader interest comes when Jean Valjean is chased through the streets of Paris and is blocked from further escape by a blind alley. These two adventures occur in dark and dank atmospheres that lend further wonder to the narration. In the detective genre, pursuer and pursued exchange bouts of good and bad luck—with naturally the ultimate victory of the "good guy," usually the detective. Hugo tries to balance the fortunes of Javert and Jean Valjean even though he must rely so much upon coincidence—more so perhaps than in the ordinary detective tale.

Hugo's technique is masterly as Jean Valjean continually falls into the grip of Javert. At the moment of Javert's triumph, on each of these occasions, the sleuth is foiled by the goodness and honesty of Jean Valjean. In fact, even a nun consents to lie to save the life of Madeleine from Javert at the end of Part I. Although *Les Misérables* would not be the comprehensive compendium of ideas and ideals it is were it to consist only of the story of Jean Valjean and Javert, such a book would still be a major contribution to the detective genre.

A STORY OF WAR AND REVOLUTION

Les Misérables is a military novel by dint of two major examples: the battle of Waterloo, and the abortive insurrection of 1832. The first description is really extraneous to the action of the novel; it has no place in the strict chronological analysis of the book. It represents a flashback on the part of the author. It does serve to explain an interesting development of the plot—Marius' devotion to the cause of the rascally Thénardier—but this alone would not be sufficient reason to justify devoting so much space to the battle scenes. However, Hugo is trying to explicate the outstanding historical event of the early nineteenth century for France—the end of the Napoleonic dream, and the starting point of a new era for France. He likewise wants to probe the causes for the cult of the Emperor which grew after Napoleon's death and was traced back to that fatal military clash.

As a piece of historical research, especially for a Frenchman writing close to the events, it is remarkably impartial and accurate. Hugo is very objective in his treatment; he praises both sides for their courage and their valor in the face of death. In details, he is highly realistic even though modern investigation may correct some of his descriptions. In outlook, Hugo is quite Romantic; he sees the hand of a fateful destiny or providence in the fall of the French. Hugo is frankly didactic and wants his countrymen to grasp this concept and grapple with its consequences. The Waterloo scenes comprise an admirable blending of historical writing and literary interpretation.

The revolution of 1832 is intrinsically important to the fortunes of all the protagonists. The battle of the barricade brings them all together, except for Cosette, who is nevertheless vitally affected by the outcome. Jean Valjean saves Marius by overcoming another temptation against Bishop Myriel's counsels, and he faces his old foe, Javert, for the last time. This time, Hugo is praising the spirit and stance of the revolutionaries; and this attitude is clearly the ambitious hope of the then exiled writer for the liberation of his countrymen from Napoleon III. It is thus logical that Hugo did not depict a victorious rebellion but one that was practically doomed from the start. He wants to inspire and encourage the French to emulate the work of these young rebels—but to be successful. Revolutions are not so easily won, he seems to say. However, there is still bravery and heroism in domestic warfare as there was in battles fought on foreign soil, as at Waterloo. And only thereby can social change be effected.

In the *Revue de Paris* of June 1829, Hugo summed up his disillusion with the contemporary situation and his ideals of progress and liberty thus: "European society is coming to its end, opinion has replaced faith, the Revolution has beheaded organized religion as it has the monarchy. America is marching at the head of civilization, with this new principle of emancipation, progress, and liberty—the future law of humanity."

The authenticity of the description of the insurrection of 1832, like the narrative of Waterloo, is well established. For these vignettes of the barricades, Hugo drew upon his own knowledge and experience directly. Of course he idealizes the participants to some extent because he is striving to eulogize the martyred cause of democracy in France. But again, he has composed a compelling and thrilling episode which at first forms a welcome respite from the slow-paced love story and the repetitive theme of the detective genre. His ability comes to the fore in the way he then skillfully mixes and resolves the three aspects of the novel.

A LOVE STORY

Love, in its several ramifications, is a basic component of *Les Misérables* if one accepts a wide definition of the term. However, the love of Marius and Cosette would comprise the obvious and central explanation of this sentiment within the work. The two lovers do not meet until almost exactly in the middle of the novel, but their meeting gives an entirely new direction to the whole narrative. Again, this procedure demonstrates that Hugo planned and executed a novel with a rather rigid structure—even if its length and digressions betray this purpose. In fact, there is no indication in the action prior to the meetings in the park that a love story will be included within the total framework of *Les Misérables*. Nevertheless, once this new aspect of the novel is introduced, it gradually supersedes all the other threads of the book.

Marius and Cosette rank among the notable lovers of all literature; their love is idyllic and idealistic, and both are enjoying a first love. Elliot M. Grant has deduced that Cosette is a portrait of Hugo's wife and also of his idealization of young womanhood in France at that time. The same critic has also come to some rather interesting—and startling— conclusions about the role of Marius in the love affair: "Marius, on the other hand, is an interesting character in whom Hugo depicts much of his own youthful aspirations and political idealism. As we saw in the first chapter, the poverty which Marius endured after his break with his grandfather resembles Hugo's own poverty in the rue du Dragon after his mother's death. When the author said of Marius' privations that 'destitution engenders greatness of soul and mind' he knew from personal experience what he was talking about. After Marius meets Cosette, he worships her in the same ultraromantic fashion that the twenty-year-old Victor Hugo worshipped Adele Foucher. The pages devoted to this idyll seem like an echo from the *Lettres à la Fiancée*. The same fervor and exaltation are present." In fact, the love story is strangely lacking in plausibility at times; the lovers never get to know each other really before their marriage. In direct contradiction to the saying that "the course of true love never did run smooth," this love between Marius and Cosette is without a ripple on the stream of marital bliss.

One jarring autobiographical note to this serene and felicitous love story may be mentioned for a revealing glimpse at Hugo's realistic nature, as Grant observes: "And yet in spite of this sentimental recollection of his courting of Adéle, Victor Hugo chooses as the wedding day for Cosette and Marius the date of February 16, 1833. Thus their nuptial night coincides with the beginning of Victor Hugo's liaison with Juliette Drouet. A strange man, Hugo." The love story is nonetheless a generous concession of Hugo's part to popular success, and the travails of Marius and Cosette are escapist devices appealing to the mass reading audience. At the same time, the whole tenor of the love story follows the pattern of Romanticism. There is nothing of the Realistic and Naturalistic schools of thought in the rendition of this aspect of *Les Misérables*. For the modern reader, the love story may be perhaps the least satisfactory element of the novel; however, one must also grant to Hugo a penetrating and beautiful glimpse into the psychology of the mental attitudes of love and of lovers.

A ROMANTIC NOVEL

It is necessary to remember that the attempt to classify *Les Misérables* into several types of the novel is arbitrary—there is an evident overlapping of the aspects of the novelistic art which defies any regimentation. Thus, the entire love story of Marius and Cosette is strictly according to the Romantic school. While the love story is a type of the genre, it is developed according to the whims of Romanticism. But *Les Misérables* is also the culminating creation of Romanticism, even though it chronologically falls after the decline of the Romantic ideal. Paul Bénichou defines it thus: "It is certainly true that *Les Misérables* is the most finished example of a technique which the Romantics preferred to all others: the development of an idea by means of a story." Even so, the plot is strongly Romantic in that it centers on the tragic existence of a solitary and unwanted individual battling fate and misfortune. The idea of course predominates, and Hugo is frankly and constantly didactic. The Romantic philosophy of optimism in the upward climb of humanity; the validity of beliefs such as humanitarianism, democracy, and charity; and the concern for the underprivileged are uppermost factors in *Les Misérables*.

In the construction of the novel, Hugo has also made use of the Romantic traits of the melodramatic, as in the numerous sufferings of Fantine, Jean Valjean, and the others; of the confrontation of opposites, such as the sharp contrast between Jean Valjean and Javert; and in the free usage of scenery, which somehow always stresses the exotic, the unusual, or perhaps the repulsive, as in the sewer episode. Therefore, the reader can hardly conclude that such swings of the pendulum of time, place, and action could have logically taken place. The novel defies the Classical doctrine of *vraisemblance,* or verisimilitude—the events probably could not have occurred. There is so vast a dependence upon the imagination that the story—while exciting and intriguing—is not believable.

This reliance upon what Coleridge defines as "the willing suspension of disbelief" certainly does not detract from the value and permanence of the novel's place in literature. And indeed the reader should be prepared to accept these imaginative and unrealistic traits against the background of Hugo's leadership of Romanticism and advocacy of the Romantic doctrines throughout his career.

A REALISTIC NOVEL

It is not contradictory to discuss *Les Misérables* as a realistic novel, although it has just been spoken of as a Romantic work, if one uses the word "Realistic" with a capital letter. Realism had succeeded Romanticism as the prevailing literary current in France just as Naturalism, led by Emile Zola, would bring an extension of the comparatively moderate Realistic themes. *Les Misérables* is a Realistic novel because the actors are taken from real life and circumstances although the occurrences that befall these characters are treated Romantically.

There is also a precise and objective enumeration of the environment, the geographic setting, the histories of the personages, the historical period, and the contemporary milieu. In fact, most of the characters are drawn from the lowest, most unfortunate classes of society, which makes the task of the Realistic novelist more forceful and influential. The dialogue in the novel reflects carefully the background and education of the participants, and Hugo is not adverse to the use of slang, ungrammatical expressions, and rough language to convey the feeling of a truthful representation of reality.

Hugo explores his minor characters with the same detailed concentration that he expends on the protagonists; and these secondary figures stand out as representative spirits of society during that era. Perhaps the most memorable portrait is that of the Thénardiers—father and mother—who symbolize the dregs of the social pool; for instance, Hugo cannot restrain himself from indicating the lamentable future of Thénardier—the rascal will use Marius' money to ply the slave trade. Many of the events and locales are even sordid and reprehensible, and more than one person on the scene is an impossible rogue—the gangsters with whom the Thénardiers ally themselves are the leading proponents of this idea of Hugo.

Critics like Edmond Benoit-Lévy have proved from extensive research into the background and genesis of Hugo's novel that the author extended his vision into the areas he would write about. Hugo visited many of the scenes he later used, and he did considerable investigation in the fields, such as industrial manufactures, he would analyze. He was not averse to inserting facts from his own experience for the sake of the esthetic ideal, and he pointedly used an actual case about a charitable prelate and a released prisoner.

Hugo's own life resembles that of Marius in not only external details but in the political searchings and in the parental difficulties. Paul Bénichou reduces Hugo's formula in this fashion: "*Les Misérables* is first of all the product of a varied experience of the world, containing the perceptions of an entire life. And this image of reality is also a realistic image. The symbol, as Hugo uses it, does not idealize things; rather, it expresses their spiritual meaning without disguising them."

A RELIGIOUS NOVEL
It is difficult to dissociate the religious and philosophical facets of such a vast novel as *Les Misérables*. For example, the two predominant themes of the innate goodness of man, and the possibility of human redemption by love and kindness, are certainly both philosophical and religious concepts. However, the novel reveals two definite features of Hugo's religious outlook: he is decidedly anticlerical, and he is against organized religion. These sides of his personality are revealed most clearly in the personalities of those who deliberately abandon the world. For Hugo, this type of existence is an anachronism in the modern age; it serves no noticeable

outward spirit, and it is an unhealthy mental condition for those who so elect it.

Although he strives to be impartial and say some good things about the anonymity and the silence to be found in cloisters, the general viewpoint is very unfavorable. There are throughout *Les Misérables* other comments, on the whole harsh, about the Church and established religious institutions. Of course, anticlericalism is not uncommon in predominantly Catholic countries, and it is important to recall that Hugo is also a child of the Enlightenment—the Age of Reason in the eighteenth century, which witnessed in France bitter attacks by writers such as Voltaire on organized religion.

Nevertheless, there is nothing contradictory in the assertion that *Les Misérables* is a religious novel; and it may be well to repeat the key sentence in the book: "We are for religion against religions." Bishop Myriel, on the surface a minor character, is truly an outstanding one because of the enormous influence which his ideas have on Jean Valjean. Bishop Myriel is based upon a real prelate of the Church in France during Hugo's lifetime. As early as 1828 or 1829, Hugo had investigated the case of Msgr. de Miollis, Bishop of Digne, who enjoyed the reputation of saintliness. As early as 1832 Hugo had the intention to make the real ecclesiastic's charity to a convict the focal point of his own novel.

Bishop Myriel is of course the ideal Christian; he is the personification and the idealization of the doctrines of Christ. Some critics even argue that as a consequence he is Hugo's claimant to the near impossibility of living up to such lofty dreams. However, Bishop Myriel also expresses many of Hugo's own notions: belief in the people, in education, in progress, and in optimism. Likewise, Bishop Myriel is a rather unusual man who accepts the unorthodox philosophy of metempsychosis (the transmigration of souls) and kneels for a blessing from an old revolutionary of 1793. Without the presence of Bishop Myriel, Hugo's religious views would not be so apparent.

Hugo believes in God and religious ideas despite his unorthodoxy, and the Waterloo digression gives him the occasion to build upon the edifice of Bishop Myriel's practical creed. In fact, one might conclude that the descriptions of Bishop Myriel are Hugo's religious points of view for the daily life of men and women, and the insights about the significance of the Napoleonic defeat represent his approach to theoretical religion. Hugo is then neither an atheist nor an agnostic; he is clearly a deist, one who believes in a Supreme Being removed from mankind. There is in history and the course of human events a certain providence, but this divine intervention—and the indefinite terminology of Hugo is indicative of his quandary—cannot be fully fathomed. Thus he can sum up the battle and its results in a striking piece of purple prose: "Such is Waterloo. But what is that to the Infinite? All this tempest, all this cloud, this war, then this peace, all this darkness, disturb not for a moment the light of the infinite Eye, before which the least of insects leaping from one blade of grass to another equals the eagle flying from spire to spire among the towers of Notre-Dame." God and Divine Will are mysteries for the Romantic which lead him toward the idealistic and the dreamy world of the imagination; the world embraces mysteries and enigmas which defy rational explication.

What then are the possible practical applications of a spiritual force in the world? On the individual plane, they can lead to a sweeping reformation of the individual who must in turn promulgate these views. Like the modern existentialists, the person is "engagé," or committed; he or she is bound to his fellow human beings and must refuse a secluded and selfish existence. Jean Valjean is part of an enormous chain reaction:

he is the disciple of Bishop Myriel who must instill these qualities in other disciples. For that reason also, Hugo has inserted so many characters whom Jean Valjean's benevolent characteristics influence. The greatest victory of this individualistic spiritual power comes in the breakdown of Javert. And Javert symbolizes more than another individual—he also symbolizes society and social strength.

Against society and social strength, against the law itself, stands a spiritual premise which can alter the course of injustice. Paul Bénichou concludes about the power of religious views or true spiritual values thus: "This Conscience above the Law was for Victor Hugo, as he wrote in several places, God himself. . . . Thus, the quartet of the Policeman, the Bishop, the Convict and the Prostitute strikingly act out the fundamental idea of *Les Misérables*: the appeal to a spiritual force in order to regenerate the social order. This force animates the entire novel, infusing it with a spirit which is as much supernatural as human. Hugo at least, let us make no mistake about it, understood his novel in this way."

But religious values must be activist, and true Christians must apply their belief in a daily context. Therefore, they cannot see their fellow comrades in Christ suffer and not rush to help. Hugo launches slashing attacks on the devout Christians who ignore the convict, Jean Valjean, in Bishop Myriel's city; on the pious citizens who fawn on Madeleine and scorn Jean Valjean in M⎯ sur M⎯; and on the ostentatious almsgiving and hypocrisy of the Gillenormands. *Les Misérables* is a religious novel in the broadest sense of the term; Paul Bénichou sees this extension of the meaning of religion in apparently unconnected vignettes: "On the one hand we have the bishop, whose charity brings back to life a dead soul; on the other there is Enjolras on his barricade, proclaiming the future brotherhood of mankind: messengers both of them, according to Hugo, of the invisible God."

A PHILOSOPHICAL NOVEL

The principal merit and intrinsic value of the manifold digressions in *Les Misérables* are the occasions that allowed Hugo to indulge in the rich vagaries of his thought. Hugo is an active reformer, and his criticisms of the existing political and moral order are intended to effect sweeping changes. Javert is the epitome of everything that is wrong in contemporary life, and Hugo is not opposed to violence for the sake of effecting his reformation. Perhaps the death of Javert is symbolic of the end of the whole nineteenth-century facade of civilization because Hugo has exposed so many unpleasant attributes of this society.

Thus, the first philosophical anguish of the author is this crying need for a radical swing to interest and concern for the exploited and dispossessed even at the cost of bloodshed. But Hugo's platform for a new order is a logical consequence of the Age of Reason and of Romanticism because republicanism, a just economic distribution of goods and services, mass education, and a progressive improvement in the lot of the common people will follow in the wake of idealism lashed to the mast of the bark of the nineteenth century. How can such a vast transformation take place? Through the acceptance of humanitarianism, charity, and goodness, says the idealistic Hugo.

Hugo can also deal with abstract principles in *Les Misérables,* such as good and evil. Evil is psychological, physical, and social; and the examples are Javert, the Thénardiers, and the outmoded system of law and order. Good can be seen on the same levels of interpretation in Jean Valjean, Fantine, and Cosette. There are of course numerous other characters who are symbols of good and evil, if not in the pure sense, then in varying degrees thereof. Throughout this novel, there is the strongest sense of sympathy for mankind; and Gavroche, the Parisian urchin, is a notable exponent of this sentiment. The novelist was an advocate of a new religion of humanity that would comprise all the above verities and would indicate a way out of the morass of the nineteenth-century environment.

Although we have attempted an understanding of the novel under its various aspects, one can reflect upon the conclusions of Elliot M. Grant about the necessity of comprehending the totality of *Les Misérables*: "So perhaps we need not worry too much about the exact classification of Victor Hugo's novel. Let us be satisfied that the book is great; great because it contains certain characters who have achieved world-wide fame, great because it reflects so admirably some of the problems and beliefs of the nineteenth century, great because it relates so stirringly certain historical events, great above all because a profound human sympathy animates its every page. Once again we discover that, wittingly or not, Victor Hugo has gone beyond the limitations of any one school."

CHARACTER ANALYSES

JEAN VALJEAN

He is not only the easily recognized hero of *Les Misérables,* but Jean Valjean is also the symbol of Hugo's concepts of goodness and love. Hugo sums up the impression of this *misérable,* great in his obscurity, when he writes: "Life, misfortunes, isolation, abandonment, poverty, are battlefields which have their heroes; obscure heroes, sometimes greater than the illustrious heroes." The redemption of Jean Valjean proceeds by four steps: the ferment in his mind after leaving Bishop Myriel with a first fall from grace in the theft of the boy's coin; the decision to save an old comrade from the galleys who is falsely accused in his place; the trip to the barricade to save Marius even though this feat will result in the loss of Cosette to her lover; and the renunciation of Cosette after the marriage to Marius.

In addition to the spiritual salvation of Jean Valjean in the four stages outlined above, there are the confrontations with Javert: the first takes place when Jean Valjean is known as Madeleine, mayor of the town and a superior to the police officer; the indirect and almost fatal encounter with the inspector when Jean Valjean is a prisoner of the Thénardiers; and the third meeting at the barricades and after the escape from the sewers. In the flight through Paris with Cosette, Jean Valjean and Javert do not actually meet one another— although both are well aware of the other's probable identity. In short, *Les Misérables* is controlled by Jean Valjean, as Paul Bénichou recognizes aptly: "And from beginning to end, through all the interruptions and innumerable subsidiary adventures, the novel develops the magnificent story of Jean Valjean, escaped convict, hero and saint."

BISHOP MYRIEL

Although the good bishop only appears briefly, if one excludes the lengthy and digressive passages on his background and philosophy, he provides the spiritual impetus which sets Jean Valjean on the right path. In Bishop Myriel, Hugo has relied upon actual facts so that the imaginative would seem to be subordinated to the realistic and biographical. However, as Elliot M. Grant notes: "The truth is that Bishop Myriel is not merely a reflection of Msgr. de Miollis, but also of Victor Hugo himself. If Myriel's career is, for the most part, like that of the benign bishop of Digne, his ideas are certainly similar to those of the novelist."

In addition to these two considerations of Bishop Myriel as a real portrait and as a representation of Hugo's thought, the prelate likewise symbolizes the ideal Christian and is the author's practical embodiment of the essential worth of the religious doctrine. The symbol of the candlesticks, Bishop Myriel's gift to Jean Valjean, is a recurring image that recalls the ecclesiastic although he is absent from further involvement in the plot.

FANTINE

Like Bishop Myriel, Fantine plays only a brief role in the unfolding drama; in fact, she does not wield the tremendous force that the prelate does. However, Fantine's pitiful state is the direct cause for Jean Valjean's skirmish with Javert initially and is likewise the reason for his solicitous inquiries and sacrifices regarding Cosette. Thus Fantine sets in motion the mainsprings of the great humanitarian outpouring of love and devotion from the hero. In addition to this immediate importance in the plot, Fantine is a representation of a common phenomenon of the times: the simple young country woman, attracted to the city by thoughts of improvement, who is seduced by callous young men. This influx from rural to urban areas was one of the major results of the Industrial Revolution.

Later, Fantine develops into another representative figure: the prostitute, victim of a pitiless society, who has a heart of gold and is really the epitome of virtue. Fantine has descended into the depths of degradation to earn money for Cosette, and Fantine is likewise a sharp reminder to the pious bourgeois how little they practice their religion. Finally, Fantine is a stock character of Romanticism: the tragic heroine, noble and good, but plagued by misfortune and the scorn of a social system.

JAVERT

Although the police inspector is the permanent force around which so much of the suspense and dramatic interest flows, he never fully emerges in his own right as a profound personality. Javert has been converted by Hugo into such an evident symbol of the hated power of law and order which ignores charity as a critique of behavior that the author does not allow him enough introspective moments in the novel. Nevertheless, when Javert appears, the reader is confronted with a memorable portrait of an individual. Javert certainly has a story to relate which justifies his conduct: he was born in prison of a convict parent; and the rationale which made him such a staunch supporter of legality is brilliantly explicated.

On Hugo's side, the cause-and-effect relationship shows a shrewd demonstration of dramatic irony and psychological cunning. The police inspector has been molded so greatly by the past that he is a pathological case; he is a monomaniac about the adherence to the legalistic code—even when it is wrong and merciless in its execution. When his defenses start to crumble because of contact with Jean Valjean, who does not fit his preconceived pattern, Javert's anguish and doubts are slowly and subtly outlined. His death by suicide is perfectly logical; he has reached a dead end by dint of his closed mind, which is unable to comprehend different attitudes. It is perhaps a pity that Javert was not accorded more space in the novel; older critics, such as Edmond Biré, centered their opinions about his characterization, whereas more contemporary writers seem to downgrade his role within the total framework of *Les Misérables*.

MARIUS AND COSETTE

So closely linked in terms of plot conception and execution, as well as personalities, are the two lovers that it would appear preferable to consider them as an entity. Baudelaire, highly critical of Hugo's mannerisms at time in *Les Misérables,* nevertheless understood his intentions about character sketches: "It is obvious that in *Les Misérables* the author wished to create living abstractions, ideal figures, each one of which, representing one of the principal types necessary for the development of his thesis, was elevated to an epic height. It is a novel constructed like a poem, where each character is only exceptional because of the hyperbolic manner in which he represents a generality." Thus, Marius and Cosette are not truly real and realistic actors in this drama; their characters are idealizations of certain basic theories of Hugo. For one thing, they serve to prove a favorite thesis of the author: the application of goodness and love will result in a forward march of humanity.

Hugo, the boundless optimist and believer in the upward course of history, sees in these two young people the fruit of the sacrifices of Jean Valjean and Fantine. One generation is yielding its place to another, but the departure of the first group should be cheerful—its work is a success. One feels more confident that Marius and Cosette will strive toward a realization of the spirit of Bishop Myriel. The lovers also serve as a light and charming balance to the unpleasant and tumultuous events affecting their contemporaries; consequently, they denote the Romantic emphasis upon the use of the serious and gay, the tragic and comic, in literature. In fact, Cosette is almost entirely a symbol of young womanhood for Hugo; seldom does she unfold as an independent personality. She is obedient—and perhaps subservient—to Marius; to Jean

Valjean she is submissive—except when her love and loyalty to Marius conflict with her feelings toward her "father." Cosette's mild and meek actions and reactions may be explained by the young age at which she first appears.

Marius, although he retains the symbolic status which Baudelaire recognized and analyzed, also has a strong autobiographical basis as well. He is specifically a reflection of the young Hugo in the thick of the fray of street battles against the Restoration; and more obliquely Marius speaks as if the author himself were uttering his opinions. At the same time, Marius is the prototype of the lover-hero of Romanticism—prepared to immolate himself on the altar of love and idealism. His devotion to Colonel Pontmercy's memory, the dubious cause of Thénardier, and the friends of the ABC political club deny self-interest; on the contrary, Marius has accepted poverty, the possible loss of Jean Valjean's needed friendship, and life itself for the sake of the causes he espouses. Then, too, Marius, like his counterpart, Cosette, is the hope of the future for Hugo: the young man will be detoured from the narrow path of smug and selfish bourgeois ambitions to the broad highway of Jean Valjean's humanitarianism.

MINOR CHARACTERS

Les Misérables, like the novels of Charles Dickens and Honoré de Balzac, offers a panoramic view of French society during the early nineteenth century with a dizzying array of secondary characters. It is not necessary to list every personage who crosses the path of one or the other of the principal figures in the novel. However, there are certain minor figures who are important in the development of the action, influence the leading characters, and explain the author's ideas.

THE THÉNARDIERS

This couple compete with each other in wickedness, cruelty, and villainy—in fact, it would be difficult to single out the more notorious of the two. The husband enters into the story in more detail, particularly after the second half of the novel, and so he perhaps gains the unwanted laurels of evil. Indeed, the Thénardiers are the epitome of pure and unadulterated evil; they reveal Hugo's feeling that sin is beyond redemption and is inexplicable. Jean Valjean carried within himself the same potentialities as the Thénardiers for a profligate life, but he surmounted temptation and succumbed to goodness. But the Thénardiers, when offered the opportunity to reform their lives, reject the occasions; they do not want Jean Valjean's help in the tavern when he takes Cosette, and they try to blackmail him when he extends financial help. Finally, Thénardier attempts extortion from Marius; and the scoundrel's disappearance from the novel is toward a bad end. With all these disagreeable features, the Thénardiers have the redeeming grace for the novelist of providing plot complications—and also plot solutions. For instance, Thénardier himself is a vital source of ironic nature for Marius' devotion to his father.

THE GILLENORMANDS
Both the grandfather and aunt of Marius have no immediate connection with the story and with the main actors; however, they go far to explain the predicament of Marius and illustrate anew the cold face of society for Jean Valjean in the last part of *Les Misérables*. The Gillenormands, particularly the grandfather, are realistic portraits of members of the "old guard" who will never accept social change; they continue to live according to the styles and political modes of the eighteenth century. Nevertheless, Hugo has shown them to be very human: the stubborn pride of old Gillenormand which rejects possibilities of reconciliation with Marius; the joy when he sees his grandson again; and the understandable hopes of the old man for the youth.

PONTMERCY
Although the brave colonel of Napoleon's armies, who was wounded at Waterloo and rescued unintentionally by Thén-

ardier, has no role at all in the story, he controls a certain part of the ensuing plot. Pontmercy by himself is a realistic and compelling depiction of a staunch follower of the Emperor Napoleon, and he may be modeled on Hugo's own father, who was a general. In the larger sense, Pontmercy represents the source of much of the adulation toward Napoleon which began to sweep France seriously after the Emperor's death and contributed to Napoleon III's seizure of power. Gillenormand, the grandfather, and Pontmercy, the father, introduce the idea of opposites very sharply: the former favoring the Bourbons and the latter the Napoleonic ideal. However, the two are sympathetic characters in their own right and are very realistically sketched.

GAVROCHE AND EPONINE
The brother and sister, children of the Thénardiers, are very similar in personality and in contribution to the novel. In fact, their deaths even bear close similarities: they die at the battle of the barricade to help Marius. Gavroche is the point of departure for a long digression on the *gamin* of Paris, and the urchin lives up to his classification by his manifold activities. Eponine is another Romantic heroine: doomed to suffer because of an unattainable devotion to a hero who does not notice her love. Eponine, as a child, mistreated the youthful Cosette—and now undergoes sufferings, albeit not deliberately, at the hands of Cosette, who is Marius' love. Gavroche and Eponine likewise represent the familiar device of Romantic opposites: the former is comical in his attitude toward life and death, and the latter is tragical and serious. They are also unusual offspring of the nefarious Thénardiers—thereby proving the perennial existence of good in the midst of wickedness.

FAUCHELEVENT
This character illustrates two points in *Les Misérables*: one technical, and the other thematic. Fauchelevent is perhaps the most unbelievable illustration—of which naturally there

are many—of the device of coincidence. Because of help rendered to an old foe, Fauchelevent, Madeleine gave the first suspicions of his true identity to Javert; and later, Madeleine found Fauchelevent employment when the latter was injured. At one of the most crucial moments of his pursuit by Javert, Jean Valjean, trapped in a blind alley, jumped over a wall—and again met Fauchelevent who in turn sheltered him. But more than a fortuitous coincidence is intended by Hugo because Fauchelevent is a decidedly changed man. He is converted by the idealism of Jean Valjean to follow the precepts of his benefactor. Thus, the adherence to Bishop Myriel's dictum has paid off handsomely: Jean Valjean has been saved as a direct consequence of his goodness. Without the help to Fauchelevent, the latter would not have been in that appropriate location now to help Madeleine. In other words, a fundamental premise of the novel is fulfilled—goodness is contagious, and man must not dwell in a vacuum but propagate his faith.

ENJOLRAS, COMBEFERRE, COURFEYRAC

In the author's words, these young men were "legitimate sons of the French Revolution . . . Enjolras was the chief, Combeferre was the guide, Courfeyrac was the center." However, these youths are also common partners of Marius; they are dissatisfied with authoritarian political rule and a rigid, unjust social establishment. All are idealistic—and not too practical—so that they prepare themselves gallantly to die for the Revolution. As much as Hugo admires and encourages this spirit as a necessary ingredient of change, he depicts the group's inability to cope with the situation realistically. A successful revolution needs courage, which the ABC club has, but it also requires an intelligent plan of operations. The author is trying through these portraits to urge upon the French under Napoleon III, and perhaps any future aspirants to progress, the way to an insurrection. Likewise, the comrades of Marius are typical of the young generation that grew up in the supposed security of the Restoration and yet rebelled against the ideas of parents such as the Gillenormands. All die heroically in the assault by government troops on the barricade when Marius is rescued by Jean Valjean.

THE *PATRON-MINETTE*

The four bandits, Babet, Gueulemer, Claquesous, and Montparnasse, dash in and out of the story; they play a particular part in the entrapment of Jean Valjean by the Thénardiers when Marius, spying on events, awaits the appearance of Javert. The gang of thugs represents the lowest stratum of society, "the great cavern of evil," which exists according to Hugo as surely as lives the visible society of the daylight hours. The gangsters illustrate pure evil, as do the Thénardiers, and for that reason, all become willing allies. They are likewise followed by Javert, proving the necessity for such an able and relentless sleuth as Jean Valjean's pursuer.

ESSAY QUESTIONS AND ANSWERS

Question
Victor Hugo writes in *Les Misérables* that "Philosophy is the microscope of thought." Comment on this statement of the author.

Answer
Victor Hugo constantly employs his feeling and talent for metaphor, a reflection of his early success as a poet. Thus he clothes his ideas in striking figures of speech. Thought refers to the myriad meanderings of the mind without any organization, and philosophy refers to the logical and rational ordering of the theories, opinions, and beliefs of a person. In short, philosophy, while it proves a guide to a coherent pattern of thought, cannot express the full richness of the mind. Philosophy is then but a segment of the depth of an individual. In *Les Misérables,* Hugo gives free rein to his imaginative thoughts. His philosophy in the novel, while apparent because of a fundamentally simple style and emphatic repetitions, is never fully organized. It is dispersed throughout the book and must be gleaned as one proceeds with the reading of the text. This mannerism is an illustration of the Romantic theory of the organic composition of a work of art: one starts with an idea and allows a spontaneous creation to pour forth from the pen. Organization implied an adherence to the classical doctrine; therefore, the Romantics asserted that they could not follow such a cold and formal procedure. In reality, *Les Misérables* is a rather well-organized volume in its totality despite Hugo's numerous digressions and philosophical analyses. Hugo labored long and hard over the novel before its publication in 1862.

Question

Compare the words of Bishop Myriel to the words and parables of the Gospel.

Answer

In the person of Bishop Myriel, Victor Hugo forcefully created a Christ-figure who practices rather than preaches the dogmas of his religion. For example, the author writes early in the first part: "In such fashion would he talk, gravely and paternally, in default of examples he would invent parables, going straight to his object, with few phrases and many images, which was the very eloquence of Jesus Christ, convincing and persuasive." In fact, the bishop preaches little; his words are limited to epigrammatic phrases; and little of his life is really known because of his simple manner. When he does speak, his words seem to resemble in form and content the words of Christ in the gospel. Many of his actions parallel in like manner the doings of Christ; for instance, he treats the poor with special concern but does not hesitate to converse with the rich in order to convert them to his ideal. His sermons are very similar to Jesus's Sermon on the Mount in the New Testament; he usually has twelve guests—a symbol of the equal number of apostles of Christ, and he travels boldly about the highways. Finally, he spends a great deal of time after the day's cares in the garden, which may symbolize the agony of Christ in the garden of Gethsemane prior to his death. And of course he strenuously advocates the course of poverty as the proper station of those who espouse love as their model; his existence supported by the kindness of others likewise denotes a resemblance to Christ in the Gospel.

Question

Verlaine, an outstanding French poet of the nineteenth century, gave this answer when asked who was the greatest poet of his age: "Victor Hugo, just the same"; and Andre Gidé, French novelist of the twentieth century and winner of the Nobel Prize in literature, answered: "Victor Hugo—alas!" What do these statements signify in relation to *Les Misérables*?

Answer

Victor Hugo made his mark as a poet before turning to triumphs in the theater and in the area of the novel; he seems never to have abandoned his poetic bent. *Les Misérables* shows distinct signs of a poetic or purple prose which adds tremendous beauty and power of the reader's impressions. Metaphors abound as do rhythmic sentences; antithesis is a favorite device; and the vocabulary is in general very rich and diversified. He transforms reality into a symbol, and he links reality to the imaginative and the mysterious.

Unfortunately, Hugo cannot restrain his exuberant nature: he is verbose and prolix, and the effect of such a hyperbolic style is at times grotesque. In brief, he fails to abide by some of the Classical doctrines of measure and balance. But no poet of the nineteenth century dared to enter the arena of the novel; and the two major novelists, Flaubert and Stendhal, wrote in a terse style, exactly opposite to that of Hugo. Yet one is unable to study the nineteenth century without considering the contributions of Hugo. The widely circulated opinions of the two French masters quoted above mean that Hugo cannot be ignored because of the quantity of writing, the influence upon the youth of his time, and the beautiful imagery of his lines. Ironically, if he had curtailed his output, he might have secured a more stable place in the opinion of critics and other poets. Less quantity might have resulted in better quality.

Question

Study the fusion of the story and of interior monologue in *Les Misérables.*

Answer

Hugo relies heavily upon dramatic or interior monologue to advance his story, and the use of the soliloquy was a favorite theatrical technique of the Romantics. Indeed, Hugo feels no qualms about interrupting the action to dwell at length on the conflicting thoughts in the minds of his protagonists, especially Jean Valjean. For example, Jean Valjean can reflect upon the agony of his situation while he is in flight from Javert through the streets of Paris. If anything, the dialogue in the novel suffers from a very noticeable reliance upon description and interior monologue; and of the three forms, dialogue is in last place. Of course, prime emphasis is awarded to lengthy description. But the interior monologue provides the practical application of conflicting ideas, such as the struggle between good and evil for Jean Valjean. One of the most effective examples of the use of interior monologue in the story occurs in the episode of Marius listening to the Thénardiers, who have Jean Valjean in their clutches. Even in the passage through the sewers, Valjean considers well his attitude; and afterwards, Hugo concentrates strongly on the lonesomeness and last anguish of his hero. If anything, Hugo is prepared to sacrifice story interest and mobility to attain a satisfaction of mental probing and a heart-rending reaction from his audience toward the character under discussion. Despite great sentimental attachment to his characters, Hugo endeavors to paint psychological doubts and queries. He is however not an objective analyst; it is always quite apparent where his sympathies are.

Question

The picture of an unhappy childhood is a common occurrence in *Les Misérables*. How does Hugo specifically draw examples of unfortunate children?

Answer

Cosette is the prime example of an unhappy child when Jean Valjean finally finds her and starts to redeem her. There is a very noticeable contrast between the treatment of Fantine's illegitimate offspring and the youngsters of the Thénardiers. Later, when Cosette is growing up happily because of care and love, the children of the Thénardiers begin to be unhappy. Gavroche and Eponine, two minor characters who figure prominently in the battle of the barricade, are practically orphans because of neglect; and their whole reaction to their environment and coming circumstances is molded by their tragic fate. Even Marius has not been immune from a sad childhood: he lives with the Gillenormands; he has lost his mother; and Colonel Pontmercy has renounced his claims as father for the son's benefit. And of course, the hero, Jean Valjean, has suffered enormously as a child; his miseries have driven him to steal bread in order to survive. In all these cases, there is a profound psychological lesson: childhood molds the adult, and youth needs kind and loving attention. This conclusion may seem trite to the modern reader, but the opinions of Hugo in 1862 were certainly somewhat revolutionary to parental concepts toward children.

Question

Les Misérables has been entitled "the novel of Paris." Discuss this opinion.

Answer

Almost all the action, and certainly the climactic events of the insurrection of 1832, occur in the French capital. Moreover, there is the geographical, political, and social employment of the Parisian environment in *Les Misérables*. Indeed, Hugo would seem to say that Paris is France. The history of Paris is given in many myriad details; the different social classes are shown; and the mentality of the people of Paris is investigated by the novelist. And Hugo is clearly not impartial in his love and exaltation of Paris! For instance, he writes this exuberant tribute to the city: "For Paris is a sum total. Paris is the ceiling of the human race. All this prodigious city is an epitome of dead and living manners and customs. . . . Paris is a synonym of Cosmos. Paris is Athens, Rome. . . . All the eras of civilization are there in abridged edition. . . ." When one recalls the enormous popularity which this novel has enjoyed, one may perhaps conclude that part of the mythic attraction which Paris has in foreign eyes may be due partly to such competent propagandists as Victor Hugo in *Les Misérables*. He also knows his city well: the names of the streets, the bridges, and the various districts of Paris are spelled out precisely. But Hugo is not interested in the inanimate objects of Paris; Paris is a symbol for the people, and Hugo takes great pride in the fact that the rebellions, and especially the French Revolution, were sparked by the dissatisfactions of the Parisian populace. Paris is therefore converted into a symbol of the revolutionary spirit and the ideal of progress.

Question

Hugo writes in *Les Misérables* that "the supreme happiness of life is the conviction that we are loved." How does the author illustrate this theme?

Answer

To Hugo, happiness does not reside in material advantages and pleasures but in the reciprocal love of human beings. Jean Valjean sacrifices everything for his idealism and Cosette's love; he dies happy because he knows that Marius and Cosette love him. Prior to the deathbed scene—which Hugo said could not fail to move the reader or otherwise he would renounce writing as a career—Jean Valjean is saddened and despondent because of the apparent rejection of his love toward Cosette and her husband. Eponine dies happy because her love for Marius, while unrequited, nevertheless is comprehended by the young man. And Fantine, in another deathbed scene, wants only the love of Cosette to blossom into a radiant creature. In *Les Misérables,* love exists on an exalted spiritual plane—a concrete manifestation of the mysterious forces which control the actions of men. For example, the only requirement of Bishop Myriel to the stunned Jean Valjean is that he return the love of neighbor by love of other fellows in distress. Thus the good prelate can live and die in peace.

BIBLIOGRAPHY

TRANSLATIONS
Hugo, Victor. *Les Misérables*. Translated by Charles E. Wilbour. New York: E. P. Dutton and Co, 1958. A one-volume edition of the same translation in paperback is published by Washington Square Press, Inc., New York, 1964. It is abridged and edited by Paul Benichou.

CRITICISM
Bishop, Lloyd. *Romantic Irony in French Literature*. Nashville, TN: Vanderbilt University Press, 1989.

Brereton, Geoffrey. *A Short History of French Literature*, 2nd ed. Harmondsworth, Baltimore: Penguin, 1976.

Bloom, Harold. *Victor Hugo*. New York: Chelsea House Publishers, 1988.

Cazamian, Louis. *The History of French Literature*. Oxford, England: Clarendon Press, 1955.

Grant, Elliot M. *The Career of Victor Hugo*. Cambridge, MA: Harvard University Press, 1946.

Houston, John. *Victor Hugo*. Boston: Twayne Publishers. 1988.

Kelley, Linda. *The Young Romantics: Victor Hugo, Sainte-Beuve, Vigny, Dumas, Musset, George Sand and their Friendships, Feuds, and Loves in the French Romantic Revolution*. New York: Random House, 1976.

Lanzen Harris, Laurie, ed. *19th Century Literature Criticism: Victor Hugo* (vol. 10). Detroit: Gale Research, 1985.

Richardson, Joanna. *Victor Hugo*. New York: St. Martins Press, 1976.

Swinburne, Algernon Charles. *A Study of Victor Hugo*. Port Washington: Kennikat Press, 1970.